PRAISE FOR
Lead Boldly

"Hugh's understanding of peak performance is a force to be reckoned with in the field of professional development."
—Mike Rice, CEO (Retired) of BioLife Solutions

"In *Lead Boldly*, Hugh's operational business experience and leadership development process showcase why he is one of the finest executive coaches I know."
—Jeff Rogers, chairman of One Accord

"*Lead Boldly* masterfully connects the dots between personal values and professional achievement, urging a journey through the pillars of loving deeply, learning daily, and living boldly. It redefines success through the lens of coaching others towards greatness and offers a compelling blueprint for fostering a mindset of continuous learning and deep connections. An essential guide for anyone committed to inspiring and achieving greatness with authenticity."
—Dr. Jennifer Brown, CEO of NorthStar Consulting

"Hugh is a masterful guide and insightful teacher, a wise confidant and powerful thought leader. He is the catalyst who helped me accelerate my leadership growth and influence."
—Dr. Bernice Ledbetter, director of
the Center for Women in Leadership

Lead Boldly

How to Coach Others to Greatness

Hugh Blane

This edition first published in 2024 by Career Press, an imprint of
Red Wheel/Weiser, LLC

With offices at:
65 Parker Street, Suite 7
Newburyport, MA 01950
www.careerpress.com
www.redwheelweiser.com

ISBN: 978-1-63265-211-9
Library of Congress Cataloging-in-Publication Data

Names: Blane, Hugh, author.
Title: Lead boldly : how to coach others to greatness / Hugh Blane.
Description: Newburyport, MA : Career Press, 2024. | Includes
  bibliographical references and index. | Summary: "This book makes the
  compelling case that there are vast levels of untapped potential in
  every corner and cubicle of organizations. Because of unparalleled
  stress, burnout, disengagement, and continual distraction, employers are
  sitting on a treasure trove of potential but have lacked the mindset and
  skillset to unlock this potential. This book provides leaders with a
  step-by-step process for becoming the person known for coaching others
  to greatness"— Provided by publisher.
Identifiers: LCCN 2024001871 | ISBN 9781632652119 (trade paperback) | ISBN
  9781632652126 (ebook)
Subjects: LCSH: Leadership. | Executive coaching. | Employees—Coaching of.
  | Management. | BISAC: BUSINESS & ECONOMICS / Mentoring & Coaching |
  BUSINESS & ECONOMICS / Management
Classification: LCC HD57.7 .B564 2024 | DDC 658.4/092—dc23/eng/20240206
LC record available at https://lccn.loc.gov/202

Cover design by Brittany Craig
Interior image by Hugh Blane
Interior by Timm Bryson, em em design, LLC
Typeset in Adobe Garamond Pro

Printed in the United States of America
IBI
10 9 8 7 6 5 4 3 2 1

CONTENTS

INTRODUCTION:
FROM POTENTIAL TO PERFORMANCE

As I write this book, inflation is at a forty-year high. There's a war in Ukraine. A pervasive sense of quiet resignation hangs like a pall over the country. And a political divide threatens to destroy the very fabric of our democracy. The level of employee engagement remains precariously low and the competition for talent has made it so that fast-food leaders have to award signing bonuses to entice people to work in their restaurants.

We are more fragmented as a people and as a nation than we have ever been. We are divided politically, socially, and economically. People are exhausted, overworked, overwhelmed, and, often, overburdened by the impact of a pandemic that threatens us all.

The term "psychological safety" is now part of the lexicon of American corporate culture. We have stopped dreaming of what's possible and of reaching for new horizons. We are focused rather on what's *not* working. We are anxious as a people and lack the impetus and motivation for positive planning and forward thinking.

Add to this the disruptive impact of artificial intelligence (AI), a transformative technology that is ushering in a radical and unprecedented rate of change the likes of which we have never seen. This technology promises to change not only what we do and how we do it but also how we relate to one another in our communities, our homes, our places of worship, and in every nook and cranny of society.

I'm a coach. I coach CEOs, entrepreneurs, and investors, showing them how to convert human potential into inspired performance. I help leaders, teams, and employees pursue their definition of greatness and flourish professionally and personally.

In my first book, I outlined a simple formula that can help businesses to flourish. I defined flourishing as growing well or luxuriantly, thriving, doing or faring well, prospering, and achieving your highest productivity or influence. When businesses flourish, they make bold, sweeping movements and take significant actions. If that definition resonates with you and you want to encourage your business or professional life to flourish, you can do that by taking three simple steps:

- Help your customers to flourish by creating services and products that delight them and make their lives better than your competitors' products do.
- Commit to enabling your employees to flourish.
- Start flourishing as a leader and become an ambassador of flourishing throughout your organization.

You cannot accomplish step one without accomplishing step two. And you can't accomplish either step one or step two without committing to step three.

So ask yourself: Are you flourishing? Read the definition again and rate yourself on a scale of one to ten by asking yourself these questions:

- Are you growing well?
- Are you thriving?
- Are you doing or faring well?
- Are you prospering?
- Are you in a period of highest productivity?
- Are you excelling?
- Are you influencing others to excel?
- Are you taking bold, sweeping actions?

The ideas presented in this book can help you to to do all these things in order to achieve your own definition of greatness.

My goal here is to help you and the people you lead, coach, and mentor to win at work and succeed in all areas of your personal lives. The path down which I hope to lead you is based on three simple principles: love deeply, learn daily, and live boldly. Each of the three parts of this book examines one of these principles and gives you practical ways to implement them.

In Part I, I make the case for returning the word "love" to the world of work. As my colleague Steve Farber once wrote: "Love is a game changer."[1] But for too long, this word has been treated as taboo in the workplace, as it's frequently thought of in a romantic sense. But the love I speak of here is not romantic or familial love. Instead, I advocate for what I believe is the highest form of love—*agape,* the love that makes you want the very best and highest good for others. It's the desire to see others flourish, even when that may not be to your own advantage. We'll examine the impact this love can have on your financial statements, your customer relationships, your employee engagement scores, and your ability to experience deeper levels of focus and flow at work.

In Part II, I offer eight principles all leaders and coaches need to learn to achieve greatness in their professional and personal lives. My case rests on the idea that, if you truly love doing something, you want to get better at it. You don't rest on your laurels. You don't coast or sit on your rear end and take things easy. You are drawn to getting better at that which you love doing, and you do that by learning daily. Whatever you love—your children, your work, a hobby—if you're on fire about it, nothing can stop you from learning about it and getting better at it. You read all you can about it, you watch videos about it, you study everything available in order to achieve your very best and to be the very best at that which you love.

In Part III, I make the argument that, when you love something and have learned about it daily, you have an enthusiasm for using that new knowledge in service of what you love. You take immediate and inspired action—not just any action, but action that is rooted in love and that is the highest and best for the people who matter most to you. There's a courageousness embedded in what you do. Boldness is rooted in confidence and courage and the willingness to take risks. You're not afraid of losing when you live boldly. If you feel fear, it's the fear of not utilizing your talents and skills in a way that pursues and achieves that which you love.

These principles have the potential to transform your leadership and the results you achieve in unprecedented ways.

Specifically, they ensure the accomplishment of five high-value and strategic leadership priorities:

- They build your reputation as an indispensable asset that produces exquisite return on investment (ROI) for your organization by coaching people to pursue their own definition of greatness.
- They encourage the building and leading of high-performance teams.
- They create a culture characterized by excellence, passion, innovation, and growth.
- They help you become a magnet for top-tier talent.
- They enable you to accomplish more with less work.

But converting human potential into inspired performance requires that you challenge long-held assumptions about coaching and its impact on business results, performance metrics, and success—both professionally and personally. To achieve elevated performance, you must articulate what you love deeply in an authentic and compelling way, commit yourself to learning about it daily, and have the will to live boldly in order to accomplish your goals.

As someone with over thirty-five years of experience coaching leaders and teams to achieve greatness in their areas of expertise, my commitment to you is simple: If you read this book, internalize its content, and embrace the context—if you implement its insights with courage, humility, and discipline—you will live a life of success as well as significance.

If you aspire to achieve greatness for yourself, as well as enable greatness in others, the chapters that follow will challenge you, encourage you, mystify you, and, ultimately, catapult you to the accomplishment of your highest hopes, dreams, and aspirations. As your coach in success, I am committed to helping you become the very best leader and coach you can be.

Love Deeply

Introduction to Part I

We don't use the word "love" in boardrooms or corner offices because we think it's too touchy-feely and doesn't have a clear line of sight to greater performance. It also makes leaders feel uncomfortable. So we relegate the word to conversations about our children, our hobbies, and our favorite restaurants, movies, and sports teams. We've allowed love to become the mainstay of our personal lives, but we don't understand the word's myriad meanings or its relevance in the workplace.

William James enjoins us to, "Let everything you do be done as if it makes a difference." We're reminded of this because what you do has an impact on others and makes a difference. Ninety-plus percent of my clients say they want to make a difference but seldom take the time to ask if their intention of making a positive difference matches their impact.

The desire to make a difference and the absence of information as to whether you are making a difference leaves you guessing and uncertain. Without some of the tools I'll share with you in this, you will, as Henry David Thoreau said, "Live lives of quiet desperation." And that is even more true today, three years after the start of a worldwide pandemic.

The love I advocate in this book is not the sappy romantic love that's written about in tabloid magazines or covered by network TV shows. Nor is it the kind of love that requires years of monastic meditation in Himalayan caves. It is a love that, when articulated in heartfelt purpose, vision, and value statements, wins the hearts and minds of leaders, teams, and customers. That kind of love makes a transformational difference in key business metrics. I've helped teams harness the power of this love for over thirty-five years. The next six chapters will show you how to do that in your own personal and professional life.

CHAPTER 1

Be a Difference Maker

That's the beauty of coaching. You get to touch lives.
You get to make a difference.

MORGAN WOOTTEN

I can count on one hand the number of people who have had a transformational impact on my life. My parents certainly did, but a very close second (and the catalyst for my professional life today) was David Litton, my junior high school track coach.

Coach Litton changed the trajectory of my life. That's not hyperbole. In a very real way, he entered the life of a skinny, troubled immigrant kid and planted the seeds of what was possible, the power of perseverance, and even the idea of pursuing excellence. I didn't possess those attributes before being coached by him, but the fact that he had planted the seeds of greatness in me is a testament to his impact.

I wasn't raised with greatness in mind. I was raised with a mindset of adversity, anxiety, and poverty by an immigrant family that was struggling to survive. My family came to the United States in 1968 with no furniture, little luggage, and great hope that we could recover from the financial reversals we had suffered in Scotland. My father's business had bankrupted our family. By the time three men knocked on our front door to repossess our furniture, we were broken financially, emotionally, and, in some ways, spiritually. For us, immigrating was not so much about moving to the United States as it was about running away from the embarrassment of having been reduced from an upper-middle-class lifestyle to one dependent on family and friends for survival. This experience left my parents rightly focused on making ends meet, but with little energy left to attend to the emotional and psychological needs of their two young children.

We arrived in Birmingham, Alabama, in 1968, five years after Bull Connor had used fire hoses on protestors and the bombing of the 16th Street Baptist Church. I entered Our Lady of Sorrows Catholic school on the same day that four African-American girls crossed the integration barrier and enrolled there. I stood on the sidewalk with fifty other students curiously watching as these girls crossed the courtyard to enter the building. On this, my first day of school in America, I experienced prejudice and the civil rights movement up-close and personal. And I found myself closely aligned with the four girls crossing that invisible barrier of belonging because I, too, was crossing into the unknown and was eager, if not desperate, to fit in with the other kids at school.

In my first two years at school, my schoolwork was well below average. I felt out of place and unable to focus. I spent more time in the principal's office than at my desk. I had a nervous and insatiable need to talk when I was told to be quiet.

In hopes of being included and accepted, I befriended other troubled kids. I found a group of boys as unfocused as I was who were rebelling against being told what to do. On a dare from one of my new friends, I stole lunch tickets from a teacher's desk and scalped them for half price. It was a simple transaction. Your parents gave you $2.00 for your weekly lunches. I'd sell you a ticket for a dollar. You kept a dollar and so did I. After two weeks, I visited the principal's office and was found to have $65.00 in cash. I thought I was entrepreneurial, but the school principal called me a thief. She was right, and I was expelled from school.

I was then enrolled in a public junior high school, where I quickly realized how much safer Catholic school had been. Here, fitting in and becoming a part of the group was a full-contact sport. I tell you all this to provide context and help you understand where my young life was headed, and why Coach Litton's lifeline changed my trajectory so dramatically.

RUNNING FOR MY LIFE

One day in gym class, the football coach lined up all the boys in a large horseshoe and instructed the two boys at the top of the horseshoe to compete in a forty-yard dash. I'm not sure if I was smart or nervous, but I counted the number of kids in front of me to see who I was going to race against. To my shock, I saw my "competitor" was Moses, the star running back on the football team. I only knew him from seeing him walk the halls of school, where kids called his name wanting to be seen as his friend. When my eyes met his, Moses was beaming with a confident and arrogant smile. From forty feet away, it was clear how much he would enjoy devouring this scrawny kid. The likely fear on my face made this all the more delicious for him.

I started brainstorming excuses for why I couldn't run. I had an upset stomach. Nope. I felt sick and needed to go to the bathroom. Nope. How about, I want my mom! Eh . . . no, that won't work. As a Catholic, I thought of the Old Testament sacrifices and felt like a lamb going to the slaughter. I believed I was going to be sacrificed by the football coach, by Moses, and by all of the other boys for the laugh of the day. There was nowhere to hide.

After ten fear-wracked minutes, I found myself face to face with Moses. I remember he had the broadest smile and the whitest teeth. He was a god, and hearing his laughter as he contemplated racing *me* was humiliating. The football coach started laughing as well, as did the other boys. Then the coach picked up his stopwatch and asked if we were ready, to which Moses responded loudly and triumphantly in the affirmative.

I had no talent or skill for running. I was good at *running away* from responsibility, but that was it. As time slowed to a standstill, I felt a physical pain of sorts standing next to Moses. I couldn't catch my breath, but I remember bracing myself on the starting line and staring ahead. At the command to go, I felt as if I had been shot from a cannon. I was running to get the race over with. I wanted the embarrassment to end. So I ran away from it and the laughter of seventy-five boys and the devouring gaze of Moses. I ran my ass off. And so did he. But over those forty yards, Moses never pulled ahead of me. Miraculously, I crossed the finish line before he did.

Think for a moment about what had happened. Some scrawny kid (and I mean scrawny!) raced and beat the star running back. Compare this to a souped-up Honda Civic beating a Porsche 911 in a quarter-mile sprint. The disbelief was palpable. Disbelief from Moses, who certainly wasn't accustomed to losing. Disbelief from the football coach, whose star running back had just been beaten. Disbelief from the other boys, because their hero had been bested. And most profoundly, disbelief from me that I hadn't lost.

The momentary "Holy smokes, I didn't lose" moment was quickly replaced with the thought that I must have jumped the gun. I must have goofed up somehow. This was confirmed when the coach barked: "Let's see if you can do that again." As we walked back to the starting line, Moses was no longer laughing, but looked confused. The other boys weren't laughing either, but asking: "Who is this kid?" I was simply wondering what had just happened.

I won the second race, although by a smaller margin than the first, which enraged the coach, who yelled that we had to race again. As we returned to the starting line, I could feel the anger radiating off Moses. After I had beaten him for a third time and was hoping desperately that there wouldn't be a fourth race, Coach Litton stepped into the fray and suggested that the football coach give some of other boys a chance to run.

TAKING THE WIN

At first, my unlikely victory over Moses didn't turn out to be a victory for me. I had alienated Moses's friends and the other members of the football team. I was too small to play football, so I was of no value to the football coach. For the remainder of that ill-fated gym class, no one spoke to me or congratulated me. I felt more and more like an outsider. I felt responsible for embarrassing Moses and, in some perverted way, for causing him pain. Aware that I had no allies and no one with whom to share my success, I spent the rest of that day trying to avoid talking about what had happened and waiting to use my newfound speed to run home.

But Coach Litton was waiting for me as I walked out of my last class. "I think you've got a lot of potential as a runner," he said. He told me that I had done something really special that day by winning three races against Moses. Then he commented that, with a little coaching and training, I could excel at running track and suggested that I join the track team. Feeling I had nothing to lose, I decided to give it a go.

This was a transformational moment for me. Coach Litton did what great coaches do. He saw something in me that I couldn't see in myself and committed to bringing out the best in me on the track. He understood my circumstances as a troubled immigrant kid, my academic struggles, and my lack of friends. He raised the bar on what I thought I could accomplish and helped me to feel a part of something special.

I'm telling you this story to illustrate how one individual can change the trajectory of another's life. Coaching, when done in the way that Coach Litton worked with me, doesn't impact just one person's life. It affects the lives of all of the people with whom that person lives and interacts.

The coaching I received from Coach Litton has shaped and informed the businesses I have run. He influenced the relationships I have with my family, my friends, and my coaching clients, as well as with the community where I live and work. He inspired me to pursue excellence and, in the process, to become the very best version of myself. He taught me a set of values and principles that still helps shape me today and that enables me to show my clients how to rise up and live abundantly. His coaching was a gift given to me at a time when I needed it the most. I now share this gift with you, as I believe that we, as a culture, are in need of it now more than ever.

QUESTIONS

As you reflect on the story of Coach Litton, think about how similar experiences you may have had in your own life have changed you—for better and for worse.

- Who are the three most influential people you've known and what did they do that changed the trajectory of your life?
- How do you pay forward what they taught you?
- How have your relationships with these people shaped your definition of greatness?

With your answers in mind, let's now take a closer look at what it means to love deeply.

CHAPTER 2

The Three Loves

Your work is going to fill a large part of your life, and the only way to be truly satisfied is to do what you believe is great work. And the only way to do great work is to love what you do.

STEVE JOBS

Before we start to explore the black-and-white financial aspects of love at work, let's first recognize that there's one core human desire that we all share—the desire to know we are loved and valued for who we are as individuals and not because of our success or stature.

When we feel loved like this, we experience a deep sense of acceptance. We live more gratefully and we extend that gratitude to others. The CEO of a $500 million firm once explained to me the impact of these feelings on corporate life:

What you're in love with, you work to preserve. You don't try and preserve things you're not in love with. I work every day to love people fully. My wife and kids? Of course. My employees? Yes. My customers? Yes. I've come to understand and work to make real the quote by Kahlil Gibran who said: "Work is love made visible."

Stop and think about the simplicity and clarity of what this CEO was saying. If work is love made visible, and if wanting your employees to love your customers and provide them with highly distinctive and differentiated experiences, having your brand and market share rise above competitors will only be accomplished with and through your employees.

But that begs the question of whether your employees feel loved and cared for. Now, you wouldn't be reading this book if you willingly set out to hurt your employees. But do you actively set out to love them?

It took me until the age of forty-seven to fully understand how important love is to success at work and in life. I was in love all right; but I was in love with one thing in particular—financial success. But the thing I loved did not create economic or enterprise value for the companies with whom I worked. It created value for *me*.

NINETY-DAY WONDER

As I described in the Introduction, my parents' financial reversal when I was six caused my beliefs about my home and family to shift radically. Where I had once felt safe and secure, I felt threatened and vulnerable. I learned that everything I held to be important could be taken from me— my relationship with my parents, my safety, and, yes, even my home and furniture. As I grew into a young adult, I committed never to experience the same kind of financial hardship my parents had—hardship that drained their relationship of love, affection, joy, wonder, and hope, leaving only obligation and necessity. Financial stress became a constant companion for them.

Because of this experience, I grew up with a scarcity mindset, and with a deep fear of ending up like my parents in my financial life and in my relationships. I lived in constant fear of losing everything and thought about money all the time. I made decisions based on whether I could make the maximum money possible. I became a serial entrepreneur, and making money was my primary focus. In fact, I was obsessed with money.

My love affair with money prompted me to look at people as ATM machines and at relationships as transactional. I didn't really love the people with whom I worked. I loved what they represented—a means to achieving financial success. I was self-focused and selfish.

Then I got a big break. At twenty-seven, I got the job of my dreams as a regional manager at a real estate investment firm, complete with the title, status, authority, salary, and confidence I craved. I was the youngest regional manager ever in the firm, and I was viewed by the investors as the golden child. I was recruited to lead the company through a period of transformational growth and was promised that I would be rewarded handsomely for doing so. This job was my big break, both in my career path and in my financial life.

The honeymoon lasted for ninety days. On the ninety-first day, I was hauled into the executive suite and told that I had angered and estranged every employee in the corporate office. I might be smart, talented, and driven, they told me, but if I didn't reverse their view of me in another ninety days, I would be gone.

I know now that I had behaved like a jerk for one reason. I believed that all my employees needed to get a life; they needed to be grateful they had a job and get their jobs done. I didn't understand what their responsibilities were or why they worked for the firm. I didn't care about their individual dreams, hopes, and desires. I was totally focused on driving the numbers and assuring the people who had hired me that they had made the right decision. Who would want to work for a jerk like that? As it turned out, no one.

This was a dramatic moment of crisis for me. I remember leaving the CEO's office knowing that each employee in the corporate office was watching me. No one made eye contact with me as I ran to my office, closed the door, and started cussing the employees for being so disloyal. The one piece of advice the CEO had given me was to go by the library on the way home and pick up a copy of *How to Win Friends and Influence People* by Dale Carnegie. I did, but I was so angry and ashamed that I couldn't read it.

This experience prompted me to reach out for help to the one person who knew me better than anyone—my mother. I told her that all I had worked for and hoped for, everything I thought I deserved, was in jeopardy. I was desperate and needed to find a way to worm my way back into the good graces of the people who thought I was a jerk. She sent me to a friend of hers who was a healthcare consultant to hospital CEOs. He listened attentively to my story, asked some thought-provoking questions, then shared his diagnosis with me.

"You love money and success more than you do people," he told me, adding that this love occupied the center of the proverbial altar of my life. The problem, he observed, was that I remained unaware of the impact that my exclusively financial focus had on others. And that impact really mattered. "You have disordered priorities," he cautioned, "and what matters most to you is on display for everyone to see." He understood that my beliefs were rooted in a scarcity mindset and why. But he warned that, no matter what I accomplished in life, it wasn't ever going to be good enough. As proof of this, he pointed out that, whenever he said something affirming or complimentary to me, I answered "Yes, but" and summarily dismissed him.

Then he asked a key question: "Do you want to make a difference in people's lives? Or do you just want to make money?" If I just wanted the money, power, and status of being a leader in this organization, he advised that I get out of the leadership game altogether.

I absorbed some of what this consultant said, because I was in survival mode and needed a way to counter the threat of losing my job and opportunities. True, I was in denial and angry; but I knew that I needed a way out of the mess. Then he outlined his remedy—a simple plan that could provide a clear path to saving my job. It consisted of three steps. First, go to every employee and apologize. Then tell them I wanted to get better and that I wanted their help. And finally, ask them for suggestions for how to improve. I needed a huge dose of humility, he told me, and warned me that, if I wasn't sincere, this would backfire. He was an exemplar of "tough love."

I went to every employee as he suggested and was as humble as I knew how to be. I wasn't perfect by any stretch of the imagination, but I walked away with suggestions for how not to be a jerk. As I followed his three steps, I was humbled and disciplined, and, over the next ninety days, I dug myself out of the hole I had created. The chairman of the board later said he never thought I'd be able to make the shift, but that people were noticing that I was trying.

This was the first baby step I took on my journey to fall out of love with money and to build a bridge to the idea that employees have hearts and minds as well as hands. The experience of my family had led me to focus exclusively on financial success. But my near failure at the job of my dreams helped me to fall out of love with money and fall in love with making a difference in other people's lives.

BABY STEPS

My first step down this path was to realize that learning about what other people love and believe is most important to them is crucial to success. I started to read about leadership, communication, workplace culture, teamwork, and the psychology of high performance. And yes, I started to search out ideas about love that later led me to a concept that became known as "disordered attachments."

Most important, I learned that there are three different words for love that come from the Greek: *eros, philia,* and *agape.* Each word means something different, and understanding these differences shaped my understanding of the relationship between love and leadership, and how we and our employees engage in work with customers, stakeholders, and coworkers. Let's take a brief look at the implications of these three different words.

Eros

Eros is the word from which the word "erotic" is derived. While it can have a sexual connotation, it's also often used to describe things we love doing or about which we are passionate. For example, you might say: "I love stand-up paddleboarding." This could refer to a number of elements that make up the experience of paddleboarding—being on the water, having the sun and smell of the water all around you, or the exercise and physical demands involved in paddling in open water or in rivers. It can also be used to describe a passionate emotion, like the love you feel for a certain kind of music, or certain movies, or your favorite meals, or the places you love to vacation. This kind of love is directed toward the people, activities, or situations you find personally rewarding. At work, it can be useful, because most leaders want their employees and teams to be passionate about their work.

In our culture today, we have misguided notions of romantic love. We frequently use the words "I love you" to describe how a person makes us feel. This type of love is rooted in the pleasure we receive from being in the presence of another person or activity. But if that person or activity is removed, the feelings of love disappear as well.

The core concept in this form of love is that it is conditional—rewarding or beneficial to us as long as the person or object is present. It is a "me-focused" kind of love. I was passionately in love with money and success, both of which can be rewarding. Although any passion rooted in *eros* can be rewarding and fulfilling if directed to a positive end, when taken to an extreme, it can have a dark, self-centered side as well.

Philia

Philia is brotherly love. It can be experienced as the friendship between members of an organization or club, or the residents of a city or town. It's rooted in a mutual connection or affection, fondness, or affiliation (a word that derives from the original Greek). This type of love responds to reciprocal appreciation and mutual respect, and even simple acts of kindness. It's a higher form of love than *eros* because of the choice that's required to participate, but it carries the risk of being compromised when challenged or under stress. Characteristics of this type of love are kindness, affection, and attraction. It's a "we-focused" kind of love.

There's nothing wrong with this type of love. Enjoy it, even savor it, as it's a part of all high-performing teams.

Agape

Agape goes above and beyond the two previous forms of love. It's a self-sacrificing type of love that is expressed on behalf of others, regardless of how close and intimate the relationship. It goes beyond natural affection. Those motivated by it do not consider the value of the person or object of the love; their actions are grounded rather in its spiritual or God-given nature. In its purest form, agape directs love toward the unlovable. It is "other-focused" and plays a significant role in Christianity as the kind of love exhibited by Christ.

In a work context, agape starts with a focus on others before focusing on the self. It's a generous and humble kind of love that's not seen in many organizations today. It is grounded in humility, a quality that has gotten a bad rap today because many view humble people as wallflowers or weak, spineless pushovers. But as C. S. Lewis so correctly pointed out: "Humility is not thinking less of yourself but thinking of yourself less."[2] So true! In chapter 7, we'll look at something I call "humble swagger," a kind of confident humility that can yield surprising results in the workplace.

All three types of love have a place in the world of work. The bottom line is simple, however: You have to stay in love with what you do if you want transformational growth. "The secret to success is to stay in love. That's the essence," John Stanford, a former military officer and superintendent of public schools in Seattle, claims.[3] You have to stay in love with the people you lead, and with the work you've chosen. When you love deeply at work, you can accomplish the extraordinary.

QUESTIONS:

Ask yourself these three questions to help you understand how these three types of love are playing a role in your work life.

- Can you state with conviction and clarity what you love about your work?

- If you typed your answer to the question above on a piece of paper and left it in a public place in your office, would it be returned to you with an acknowledgment that you dropped something?
- What is the one idea, dream, hope, or aspiration you have for your work?

If you are having trouble answering any of these three questions, perhaps the discussion of how love fosters greatness in chapter 3 will help.

CHAPTER 3

Love Fosters Greatness

Whatever you can do, or dream you can, begin it.
Boldness has genius, power, and magic in it!

GOETHE

What do Tom Brady, LeBron James, and you have in common?

Over the course of a week in 2023, two significant events transpired in the world of professional sports. First, Tom Brady retired for the second time at the age of forty-four after twenty-three years in the NFL. Brady had been chosen in the sixth round as the 199th overall draft pick—a low position. His career in the NFL was seen as a long shot, to say the least, yet he retired with seven SuperBowl victories and five SuperBowl MVP player awards—the most ever for each of those categories. No one ever thought that a slow, skinny kid from the University of Michigan would collect a record number of awards and accolades. But today, Tom Brady is called the GOAT, the Greatest of All Time.

Just a few days later, LeBron James became the leading all-time points-scorer in the NBA, having scored 38,390 points,

surpassing Kareem Abdul-Jabbar. And he did so having
played two years fewer than Abdul-Jabbar. LeBron's awards
and MVP status are exceptional, including NBA MVP of
the Year award, four NBA championship titles, ten NBA
championships, and many others. Oh, and his net worth is
estimated at $1 billion! Yes, that's one *billion* dollars.

BECOMING THE GOAT

I'll leave the debate over applying the moniker GOAT to
Brady and James to others. What I want to suggest here is
that these two world-class athletes are incredible examples of
the three principles addressed in this book. Their lives point
us in the direction of the excellence anyone can achieve,
regardless of their professional field—whether education,
finance, technology, community-building, or civic action.
When internalized, these three principles can have a real and
tangible impact on our normal, everyday lives. Brady and
James have three things in common that anyone interested
in pursuing greatness for themselves or enabling it in others
can use to succeed: they love deeply; they learn daily; and
they live boldly.

Let's take a brief look at how each of these sports icons implemented these principles in their careers and in their lives.

Loving Deeply

Brady loved the game of football, and James continues to
love the game of basketball. They didn't just *like* their respective sports; they were *passionate* about the game, the

competition, the preparation, and the camaraderie with other players. They loved the grind—daily pursuing greatness without ever faltering.

Although I have never spoken to either of these players personally, their commitment to and love for their sports comes through clearly in interviews and articles. Their public statements and actions demonstrate how their passion for their sports helped them pursue and accomplish unimaginable results and success. Climbing to the pinnacle of any endeavor—especially in the ultra-competitive world of professional sports—requires a passion that surpasses any and all difficulty, injury, career change, or hardship.

As an eighteen-year-old kid fresh out of high school, James played for the Cleveland Cavaliers. When asked about his goals in the NBA, his response was simple: "I want to be the greatest basketball player in history."[4] With striking boldness and audacity, he simply stated that he wanted to be the greatest one ever to play the game. Tom Brady also clearly stated his intention to be the best. It's only in hindsight, after twenty-plus years of witnessing their greatness, that we can now see the connection between their excellence as players, their love of their sports, and their bold proclamations as young men. They love deeply.

Learning Daily

Tom Brady was known for watching tapes of his opponents on the field. He devoured video footage and pushed his video production team to provide him with more and more high-quality footage. He knew instinctively that, if he wanted to be the greatest in his sport, he couldn't rely on his talent alone. He needed to work harder and longer than his competitors, approaching each game believing that he knew as much—if not more—about how his opponents would respond to his play-calling than they did.

LeBron James also had a hunger for learning. In a conversation with one of his coaches, he acknowledged that, to be the greatest ever to play the game, he had to improve his three-point shooting. The coach told him that excellence in the game started with excellence in visualization and practice time, and together they outlined a three-step plan for improvement:

- Hire a three-point shooting coach (yes, there are such coaches).
- Make 200 three-point shots off the dribble every day, and another 200 catch-and-shoot three-pointers, both while imagining the best players in the league defending him.
- Have the team videographers make an eight- to twelve-minute highlight video of him making three-pointers to help him internalize the positive feelings he experienced when he successfully made those shots.

James commited to implementing this plan while playing a rigorous schedule of eighty-two games per season. By adhering to it, he increased his three-point shooting from 29 to 40 percent.

There are those who love their game or profession, and those whose work ethic falters like an unreliable wireless network—on some days, off others. But those who pursue greatness never take a day off, never give less than their all on any play. They believe that the way they perform when they are tired is the way they will perform on every play. They're 100 percent focused 100 percent of the time. They learn from every practice, every video session, every play, every conversation with a fellow player or coach. They are sponges for insights as to how to be great. They learn daily.

Living Boldly

My experience of working with transformational leaders has taught me that boldness is not a behavior undertaken on its own accord. Boldness is the result of loving something so deeply that you *want* to—or, dare I say, are *compelled* to—learn about it every day. Loving and learning are not something you can turn on and off. It's hardwired into your love of an idea, a dream, a hope, or an aspiration; it's present in your DNA. When the double helix of loving deeply and learning daily are combined, the result is a life characterized by boldness, by courage, and, yes, by greatness. And we see this clearly in the lives of Brady and James.

EMBRACING GREATNESS

So I ask again: What do you have in common with Tom Brady and LeBron James? It's probably not their football or basketball skills. Most of us will never be great at football or basketball. But we all have something at which we can be great—something that resides deep inside our hearts, our minds, and our souls that, when acknowledged and expressed, will cause the people who matter most to us to say:

"You are great at that." And that perceived greatness can help you become someone who makes a difference in the lives of others.

The question I ask you here is not an easy one to answer, especially after three years of a worldwide pandemic. Why? Because, when you answer with clarity and conviction, you then have to answer the next hard question: Do you aspire to greatness in a way that drives you to embrace the discipline and "grind" needed to be as great as LeBron James and Tom Brady? That's hard to do. But, as Dan Sullivan of The Strategic Coach once said: "All progress starts by telling the truth."[5]

If you aspire to achieve greatness for yourself, as well as enable it in others, the process of loving deeply, learning daily, and living boldly may challenge you. Or it may encourage you. Or it may mystify you. But ultimately, it will catapult you to the achievement of your highest hopes, dreams, and goals. My intention in this book is to help you clarify what matters most to you so you can achieve and maintain a wildly successful life at work and a deeply satisfying life at home.

This book is about committing to living boldly and pursuing great dreams and aspirations. As William Hutchison Murray, Scottish mountaineer, wrote:

Until one is committed, there is hesitancy, the chance to draw back, always ineffectiveness. Concerning all acts of initiative (and creation), there is one elementary truth, the ignorance of which kills countless ideas and splendid plans: that the moment one definitely commits oneself, then Providence moves too. All sorts of things occur to help one that would never otherwise have occurred. A whole stream of events issues from the decision, raising in one's favor all manner of unforeseen incidents and meetings and material assistance, which no man could have dreamt would have come his way.[6]

For most of you reading this, the journey from where you are to where you want to go is currently more theoretical and less tactical or behavioral. But hopefully you will agree that you can't achieve greatness tomorrow if you aren't training for it today.

If you're waiting for a lightning bolt from the sky or an insight so penetrating that there's no way you can ignore it, that's probably not going to happen. Greatness starts with you naming and claiming the one idea, hope, dream, or aspiration that inspires greatness in you. So what is it that you love so much that it inspires you to commit yourself to greatness?

QUESTIONS

Here are five questions you can use to determine whether you are loving deeply.

- Can you articulate what you want to be great at accomplishing?
- When you visualize yourself achieving greatness over the next three to five years, what does it look like?
- What are the four or five standards for greatness in your current role? How do you stack up?
- What have you done today to become even 1 percent better than you were yesterday?

- What have you done in the last ninety days that can help you be great at what you love?

In the next chapter, we'll examine the importance of knowing what you really want in life, and how that contributes to your ability to achieve greatness.

CHAPTER 4

What Do You Really, Really Want?

That which we envision and create in our mind's eye precedes physical creation.

STEPHEN COVEY

When my wife, Alyson, and I went to our favorite neighborhood restaurant the other night for dinner, our waitress walked up and asked us what we wanted. It was a simple question, one that didn't require a great deal of consideration. But it reminded me of the number of decisions we have to make every day.

What time we will get out of bed? Will we work out before going to work or have coffee before going to the gym? What radio station will we listen to in the car? What clothes will we wear? What will we have for lunch and what plans will we make for the weekend? At work, we make so many decisions that, when we arrive home and are asked what we want for dinner, we often reply: "I don't know. What sounds good to you? I'm tired and can't decide." Psychologists call this phenomenon "decision fatigue," a term that describes a state in which, after making a multitude of decisions, large and small, we lose our capacity to decide.

But deciding what you want for dinner is a significantly smaller question than the one asked in the title of this chapter: What do you really, really want, in both your personal and your professional life? In this chapter, we will double down on the responses you gave to the questions at the end of chapter 3 and try to find out what you really, really, *really* want.

THE RIGHT QUESTIONS

If you struggled to answer the questions at the end of the last chapter, you're not alone. Many overscheduled leaders think that questions like these are existential and are best left to therapists and self-help authors. But the truth is that, when we are overscheduled and lack the white space to think deeply, we don't ask these types of questions and end up living an accidental life as opposed to a purposeful one. In this context, the statement by Stephen Covey found at the opening of this chapter—that what we create in our minds affects what we create in our lives—renders the question of what you really, really want extremely important. This is both liberating and exciting.

But let's not confuse deep desires with superficial ones. The list of things we want is never-ending, and we are constantly fed information that increases our appetite for more and more things. But there's a difference between wanting a new pair of running shoes or wanting to lose five pounds, and the desires of your heart.

When I was thirty-eight years old, I met someone who prompted me to ask myself what I really wanted. A friend of mine invited me and a group of five other business leaders to meet Michael Gladych, a psychotherapist who had had a profound impact on his life. "He asks great questions about what's important to you," my friend said, "and sometimes the questions make your head hurt."

When we walked into Michael's office, we were met by a man in his early seventies with a full head of white hair, piercing blue eyes, and an almost ramrod-straight spine. He waddled as he walked, as if he had suffered an injury of some kind. He told us a little about himself—his Polish heritage, his psychotherapist father who had been a friend of Sigmund Freud, his experience as a fighter pilot in World War II, the paralysis he had suffered after having been shot down for a fourth time during the war, and his subsequent recovery, which was driven by an uncompromising belief in the capacity for greatness in the human mind and an unshakeable commitment to overcoming his physical injuries. As he spoke, I found myself impressed by how powerful he was and committed myself to return and talk to him one-on-one.

When I showed up the following week, however, Michael had a different agenda. His first question was: "Why are you here?" When I told him I had returned because of the story he had told about his past experiences, he thought for a moment then said he wanted to ask me three questions that might help to create a framework for our conversation. I agreed.

"First," he said, "who are you?"

I answered by telling him I was a native-born Scot who emigrated to Canada and eventually ended up in Birmingham, Alabama, in 1968. Then I told him about my professional experience.

"And what is your purpose for being on the planet?" he responded.

Well, this question stopped me in my tracks. I don't remember specifically what I said. It was probably similar to my answer to the first question, but much more rooted in my professional life. I was a consultant, a coach, and a business owner who was responsible for growing my business. All this sounded as if I were reading my social-media profile, and, frankly, it didn't sound like a very inspiring answer, even to me.

"And what are you doing on a daily basis to pursue your purpose on this planet?" he countered.

I looked at him for a moment, then replied that I didn't think my answer to the second question had been very profound, so any answer I gave to the third would be totally made up. Sensing my level of discomfort, he asked me if I thought it might be helpful if I asked him the same three questions. Feeling as if the governor had stayed my execution, I responded with an enthusiastic "yes" and asked him who he was.

Sitting erect on the edge of his chair, he said without hesitation: "I am a child of God. Not in a theological or dogmatic way, but I believe that I am connected to something far greater than what you and I can see or perceive on this earthly plane." Of course, a red flag went up in the competitive and comparing part of my brain that warned me that his answers were going to be way better than mine! But I forged ahead with the second question.

When I asked Michael his purpose for being on the planet, he replied: "I am here to alleviate human suffering." When I asked him what he was doing on a daily basis to accomplish that, he replied: "I give away 75 percent of my services for free. The other 25 percent is enough for me to live on." And then he just stopped talking.

He didn't say a word; he just looked at me. I felt time slow down and it seemed as if Michael's eyes bored a hole into my head. I felt like a cat on a hot tin roof who couldn't find a cool spot to escape from the discomfort of the searing heat. My mind was racing at full throttle, and I had no seat belt keeping me safe. I asked myself what I was doing there, and what was the point of these questions. What was likely only seconds seemed like minutes, and Michael never took his eyes off me and never said a word.

Finally, he broke the silence: "Maybe the reason you're here is that you want answers to these three questions. What do you think?"

My first thought was to run for the hills, but I recognized that the questions Michael had asked were important, and that their answers could be helpful and beneficial. A part of me just wanted to leave. But somewhere deep in my heart and soul, I knew that something was missing. And the next words out of my mouth were: "Yes, I think those are questions I'd like to answer." Immediately, Michael stood up, extended his hand, and said: "Excellent, I'll see you next Saturday morning." Then he walked me to the door and said goodbye.

For the next eighteen months, I worked with Michael each week to answer those three questions. Others might have answered them more quickly, but for me the work took longer. At the end of eighteen months, Michael wished me the very best and kicked me out of the nest.

THE RIGHT CHOICES

We have all had experiences with a mentor or a coach or a leader who changed the trajectory of our lives. For me as a young boy, it was Coach Litton; for me as a young adult, it was Michael. Both helped me navigate confusing questions about my own desires and ambitions, my own worthiness, and my own failure to pursue my own best life. Both helped me redefine my feelings of self-worth and understand my fears about being and doing enough. In a way, I am a living legacy of both these men. They taught me that the messes in my personal and professional life could become my message, and that I could share that message by advising and coaching leaders and teams.

Of course, the path to living a bold and audacious life is never a straight and smooth highway, and it's never mapped out with precision and perfection. Life is messy, and our confidence grows as we experiment and take risks aligned with what matters most to us. But these two mentors also taught me that living out our deepest desires doesn't require years of seated meditation and introspection. We start by saying "yes" to a vague idea of what our desired future is and clarify it as we go.

Taking a stand for what you really want and what matters most to you is a radical departure from what we experience most of the time in the workplace. Taking a position of either loving what we do or doing what we love separates us immediately from 90 percent of the people at work. Most employees merely tolerate having to work to earn a paycheck and lack the ingredients of discretionary performance. And working with these coworkers can suck the life out of us and leave us believing that naming what we really, *really* want will be met with indifference and frustration.

If you have been living a lukewarm and timid life for too long, as I was, the idea of loving deeply, learning daily, and living boldly may not feel like part of your DNA. But rest assured that the jumping-off point for living boldly is rooted in the act of articulating and clarifying what it is that you really, really want.

David Whyte warns that, in pursuit of the truest kind of love, we will walk across any territory and any darkness to take the one hand that belongs in ours.[7] But this is a solitary activity of significant proportion, one that has to be undertaken in order to do brilliantly that which only you can do and to have your heart and life set on fire in the process.

So you have a choice to make. You can live your professional and personal life in exactly the same way that you have for most of your existence. Or you can choose a different, bigger, better future. The choice is yours. But where do you start?

QUESTIONS

Take Michael's three questions, record your answers, then share them with a friend you trust and respect. Or pull out your phone, turn on your camera, and record a short sixty- to ninety-second video of yourself answering them. If you send me your video, I'll respond with additional insights and suggestions.

Sound scary? That's why we're moving toward living boldly!

In the next chapter, we'll discuss how to craft a leadership purpose that resonates with what you really want, and that can start you down the path of being wildly successful at work and deeply satisfied with life.

CHAPTER 5

The Case for Wholeheartedness

The greatest use of a life is to spend it on something that will outlast it.

WILLIAM JAMES

The word "wholeheartedness" strikes me as being a lot like the word "love." We don't hear it that often. We know what it means, but when I ask people to expand on that meaning and consider what the word means to them, I often find that they respond by explaining the opposite of wholeheartedness—which is halfheartedness. My father could speak eloquently about halfhearted effort when he watched me cut the grass as a twelve-year-old. I didn't like yard work, which means that my discretionary performance was at a very low level. My approach to cutting the grass was to complete the task in the shortest amount of time possible, and with the least effort. In the workplace today, we call this a case of JDTM: Just Doing the Minimum.

After three years of a worldwide pandemic, we've seen significant levels of inflation, uncertainty in the economy and financial markets, global conflicts, significant layoffs in the technology sector, and then a dramatic war for talent. Just doing the minimum for customers is no longer acceptable, but many employees find that their hearts are no longer in their work—whether that means a particular project, a process, or even a relationship. Many just don't have the heart for it. In Part II, we'll see this malaise expressed in what's called "the 80/20 rule," which recognizes the fact that only 20 percent of our efforts produce roughly 80 percent of our outcomes. This disparity between effort and outcome occurs when we don't commit wholeheartedly to eliminating mundane and unproductive activities from the workplace and from our relationships. In this chapter, we'll look at this phenomenon from the perspective of wholeheartedness.

In this context, the 80/20 rule is not just a nice idea, but rather an imperative if you want customers who are wholeheartedly committed to your products or services. When they're halfhearted, you're vulnerable to competitors coming in and taking your business. When they're halfhearted, you become more of a vendor than a partner—a cost center that needs to be minimized. As a vendor, you will be under continuous pressure to reduce your fees and make concessions. Partners, on the other hand, are seen as profit centers worthy of investment. Partners are often at the decision-making table discussing strategic initiatives and helping craft their customers' priorities and strategies for accomplishing those priorities.

THE BELIEF BUSINESS

As coaches, we are in the belief business. Regardless of what title you have on your business card or in your email signature, underneath that title, write Chief Belief Officer. In that role, you shape what people believe is possible, and whether team members are playing to win versus playing not to lose. As the CBO, remember that beliefs are emotional. People make decisions emotionally, then justify them logically.

I recently read about an effort by one airline to innovate their boarding process. Boarding one of their 737s took approximately forty minutes. The airline set a goal of eliminating five minutes from that process and gave an innovation team the task of deciding how to cut out that time.

There were several aspects of loving deeply ingrained in this effort. First, there's the passion for process improvement that motivated the company to recruit the brightest and best employees for the team in the service of operational efficiency. In turn, these employees were passionate about the opportunity offered. When asked what they loved about their work, they answered with conviction in less than thirty seconds with responses like: "We can remove a lot of waste, redundancy, and failure work, which removes unnecessary friction and under-performance." Some expressed their passion for improving the customer experience, while others prided themselves on the fact that they could improve the financial well-being of the airline, thereby freeing up resources to invest in other areas of the business. Many simply claimed: "Our customers will be happy to have a more streamlined process and continue to make us their airline of choice."

A number of strategies were implemented to get people boarded more quickly. One insight came from theme parks, where the sheer volume of people waiting in line to get on the most popular rides provided a perfect example of how to manage a boarding process. Reaching out to these strategies was both pragmatic and courageous. Any endeavor that requires innovation or some form of transformation must be driven by a curiosity and commitment to break away from the gravitational pull of current ways of thinking in order to see new possibilities. This skill is much in demand in many organizations.

In any undertaking requiring innovation, the people tasked with the job must have the heart for the endeavor. At the risk of sounding redundant, they have to *fall in love* with the idea. When love is present—whether a love for process improvement, or a passion for creating a team that will innovate and transform, or an ardent commitment to enhance customer experience—we as coaches and leaders have to set the stage for loving and learning in substantive ways. And all organizational transformation starts with individual transformation.

In a recent interview, English poet David Whyte recounted how, as the executive director of a nonprofit, he was busy with constant meetings and doing work that others would have described as significant and important. But that's not what David really wanted to do. He wanted to be a poet. So one day while being pulled in many different directions but harboring his strong desire to be a poet, he opened a conference-room door and asked his team members: "Has anyone seen David?" The issue was that he was the only David in the office.

In his frustration, David reached out to a friend who was a Catholic priest and asked him to come over that evening and talk with him about exhaustion. Sitting across from one another with a bottle of single-malt whiskey between them, his friend gave him a curious look and saw the sincerity in his eyes. After pondering for a few moments, the priest looked at David and said: "David, the antidote to exhaustion is not rest. It's wholeheartedness."[8] Bingo!

By the time this book is published, we will have experienced four years of a worldwide pandemic, high inflation, and myriad social and cultural pressures—all pulling at the fabric of our lives and culture. Many employees have started to question and perhaps even second-guess their decisions about how they want to spend their professional lives. Many may have found a rhythm that is both effective and productive in working from home. And yet, corporations are requiring people to come back into the office. And that requirement has prompted many to ask whether that way of living and working is how they want to work and live their lives moving forward.

Since individual transformation is the precursor to organizational transformation, let's start with you.

- On a scale of one to ten, how wholeheartedly are you engaged in your work?
- Are there parts of your job in which you're only half-heartedly engaged?
- As a leader and a coach, how wholeheartedly are your employees engaged with work?

All of your answers will be subjective, of course, but great coaches ask great questions. Maybe these can be helpful for you.

WORK AS A LOVING ACT

After David Whyte recounted the story given above, he recited his poem, *The Truelove*. The poem was inspired by a request from a group of nuns for David to speak to them about the biblical parable of the disciple Peter stepping out of a boat and walking on water toward Christ.

Poets give us a gift, even when we are not aficionados of poetry. You may not have any poetry on your bookshelf, and you may not have read a poem since high school. But we can all recognize a deep reservoir of insight in this poem that gets to the heart of the matter of love and wholeheartedness. The poem may even serve as a catalyst for your own transformation.

I ask that you read this poem in its entirety first, and then I'm going to ask you to read it again with a twist.

The Truelove

There is a faith in loving fiercely
the one who is rightfully yours,
especially if you have
waited years and especially
if part of you never believed
you could deserve this
loved and beckoning hand
held out to you this way.

I am thinking of faith now
and the testaments of loneliness
and what we feel we are
worthy of in this world.

Years ago in the Hebrides
 I remember an old man
who walked every morning
on the grey stones
to the shore of baying seals,

who would press his hat
to his chest in the blustering
salt wind and say his prayer
to the turbulent Jesus
hidden in the water,

and I think of the story
of the storm and everyone
waking and seeing
the distant
yet familiar figure
far across the water
calling to them,

and how we are all
preparing for that
abrupt waking,
and that calling,
and that moment
we have to say yes,
except it will
not come so grandly,
so Biblically,
but more subtly
and intimately in the face
of the one you know
you have to love,

so that when
we finally step out of the boat
toward them, we find
everything holds
us, and everything confirms
our courage, and if you wanted

to drown you could,
but you don't
because finally
after all this struggle
and all these years
you don't want to any more
you've simply had enough
of drowning
and you want to live and you
want to love and you will
walk across any territory
and any darkness,
however fluid and however
dangerous to take the
one hand you know
belongs in yours.[9]

Now read the poem again. This time, underline or highlight the passages that strike you the most. Then read the first stanza again, but replace the word "one" with the word "work."

There is a faith in loving fiercely the work that is rightfully yours, especially if you have waited years and especially if a part of you never believed you could deserve this loved and beckoning work held out to you this way.

The idea of a loving hand held out to us in the form of our work was David's gift to me, and I am grateful. It is just one way in which David acted as a mentor to me. This idea has shaped my thinking about the decisions I make with regard to my work and has helped me realize that there are aspects of my work that can be transformational for me, as well as for my clients.

This poem also asks us to recognize that sometimes when we are in a storm, there's a figure far across the water calling to us. This figure is the work life we know in our hearts is possible, but that we have not been courageous enough to pursue.

Just as in the parable, there's a point when we will have to step out of the boat of the known, safe, and comfortable, and go toward the kind of love that is life-changing. But it's not going to happen with a bolt of lightning. It's going to come more intimately. It comes when we return the word *love* to our work life and seek the face-to-face experience of wholeheartedness.

QUESTIONS

Consider these four questions about the idea of work being a loving act before you move on to the next chapter.

- Do you believe in the idea of work being a loving act for your customers and for you?
- Is your work life characterized by stormy seas or dry land?
- On a scale of one to ten, how much struggle is there in your professional life?

- Are you willing to walk across any territory to take the one work that will bring you fully alive?

In the next chapter, we'll discuss the actions required to make work a loving act.

CHAPTER 6

Love Is a Verb

Love is not a feeling. Love is an action, an activity.

M. SCOTT PECK

Talk is cheap. We've all heard that admonition before. It points to a critical realization that love is, in fact, a verb. Our words make a difference. They live in the fertile soil of our imaginations, as well as in the memories of our listeners. But, perhaps most important, they shape what we do and how others respond.

In fact, behavior is a form of communication. What you do expresses what is most important to you and turns the words you use into promises. We all make promises, some of which we keep. We make promises to ourselves—to go the gym four times a week, or to eat a healthy diet, or to lose weight. We make promises to our families—to be home in time to watch a child's baseball game or to help around the house. We make promises to our customers, our bosses, and our shareholders to increase the value of an enterprise over time.

We make promises to our spouses or life partners when we exchange vows that communicate a commitment to do certain things in service to the other person. In this context, love is very much a verb. It's an action we undertake to fulfill those commitments and promises. In the professional world, we have metrics to help us measure and manage our promises. We actively take steps to increase the effectiveness of a situation or process. Unfortunately, however, we have no means in place for measuring or managing our effectiveness with regard to the most important commitments of our lives—the promises we make to our partners and loved ones.

Imagine that on your anniversary you asked your spouse or partner this question: "When I made my vows to you, I promised to do these things. How have I done over the last year? What two suggestions can you give me for getting better at living out my vows?" Now imagine that you asked your best customers the same question each year: "We said we would do A, B, and C. Over the course of the last year, how have we done? What two suggestions do you have for us to become more effective in living out the promises we made to you when you became our customer?"

This chapter is not intended to provide marriage counseling. Nor is it intended to provide the only valid path for achieving market differentiation. But it's important to remember that, in a business relationship or transaction, promises are made and the long-term success and profitability of your employees, your customers, and your stakeholder relationships are connected to your ability to live in ways that bring those promises to life.

DOG-CRAZY

You can tell a lot about people by observing their behavior when they think no one is watching. Recently, I saw my wife through a large picture window looking down at our four-year-old giant schnauzer, Remy. She was talking to him and, of course, he was listening to her intently. Her face was animated and she was smiling broadly. I could tell what words and the tone of voice she was using. Likely, she was saying: "You are such a good boy. You're so sweet. You're the smartest boy."

Alyson has a deep love, respect, and admiration for dogs. If you were to see her interacting with them, you might even describe her as "dog-crazy." And you'd be right. She is a great example of the fact that love is a verb. She embodies the idea that you must act lovingly toward the things and people you love. Alyson is involved with Remy in nose work, tracking, and, at times, obedience work, because she knows how much joy he gets from these activities. She researches and reads about them voraciously, and has hired a coach to help her to be a better dog mom to Remy. And this is love in action.

THE SEVEN "Cs"

In all important relationships, love as an action consists of seven components: clarity, commitment, courage, consistency, community, confidence, and competence. Let's look each of these in detail.

Clarity

As we saw in the last chapter, it is essential to be clear when articulating your ideas, your dreams, your hopes, and your aspirations if you want to fulfill them. You have to be clear about *what* you love first, and then have clarity about the reason why this is so important to you. You have to name the love that animates you and acknowledge why it matters to you. And the *why* is important. I love the idea of converting human potential into inspired performance, because far too many people live lukewarm lives. They're timid, living a large portion of their lives in fear. I did this myself for much of my life. I'm now eager to do something that transforms living in fear into living boldly!

Commitment

Love requires commitment. Without commitment, there's hesitancy and, as W. H. Abraham cautioned, the chance to draw back. The love that serves for-profit businesses best is to love customers or employees in a way that brings out the very best in them. Unfortunately, the commitment most often expressed at work is a commitment to results—hitting quarterly performance numbers or keeping investors happy. These are real and essential goals. But they are outcomes, not inputs. Increasing net profit by 15 percent may be essential for business reasons, but it doesn't stir the hearts of employees to give their very best. But if you give your employees *your* very best in service of helping them achieve *their* very best, you're significantly more likely to achieve your very best results.

I read a story of two high school students who wanted to enter the sneaker business and bought a $10,000 truckload of sneakers. When the shoes arrived, they stood in the drive-way looking at them. One student turned to the other and said: "I guess we're in the shoe business now, aren't we?" They had just hit the point of no return. That's commitment.

Courage

We can't separate the word "love" from the word "courage," because loving is a courageous act. There is always the risk that the love we extend won't be returned, or that our hoped-for love might be seen as a weakness or vulnerability to be exploited.

But all important relationships require a willingness to be vulnerable, a willingness to extend ourselves in ways that may not be reciprocated. That's why love can be scary, be-cause it makes us feel as if we're out of control. When we feel vulnerable, we become protective and close ourselves off from the perceived threats.

There's something about entrepreneurs that makes them different from other professionals. Successful entrepreneurs arrive at a point in their professional lives at which they can't turn back. They have an idea for a business or endeavor and say to themselves and their families: "I must make a go of this. I must give this a try." Sometimes they even mortgage their homes or borrow against their retirement funds. But no matter what, they're all in. There is no hesitancy. And this is living boldly.

As we'll see in Part III, living boldly is also a courageous act that requires moving beyond the safe, comfortable, and known into that disquieting place of vulnerability and un-certainty. But courage is where true learning takes place.

We can't learn anything by repeating what we've done in the past. We have to experiment, take risks, and do things differently.

Consistency

Consistency is linked to two important words in our professional and personal relationships—trust and respect. Without these, our relationships become transactional and we waste a lot of mental energy calculating what can be expected of and from us. Without trust and respect, our actions are rooted in concerns about personal safety.

Trust is about reliability. Can I rely on you to do what you said you would do? When trust is in place, our mental faculties can be devoted to creative and innovative work. People are willing to experiment and take risks only when those who lead them are trustworthy.

Respect is about your talents and skills, and the regard others have for them. If I respect you, your talents and skills are admirable to me and I know you have what it takes to do the work that matters most.

Imagine hiring a contractor who says he will arrive at your home on Friday morning at 8:00 to begin work. But Friday morning comes around and by 8:20, the contractor is still nowhere to be found and is not responding to your texts or calls. How would you react to this inconsistency? Well, you'd likely have one answer if you'd already paid him and had a "sunk-cost" attitude. Or you might tolerate the delay and work to reschedule the job. If you are just interviewing him for the job, you might surmise that this is how he operates and choose to find another contractor. If this is the fourth time this has happened, you might lie in wait to give him a double-barrel of your love.

When commitments are made and kept, your credibility goes up. But your credibility and trustworthiness are damaged when you commit to something and don't do what you say you will. This is extremely important between leaders and their teams, and between any two people working toward a mutually desired future.

To be effective, trust and respect cannot be expressed sporadically. For people to trust and respect you as a leader, they need repeated chances to observe your communication and behavior. And it's essential for your customers or employees to trust and respect you in order for greatness to be achieved.

Community

Greatness is never achieved alone. We cannot approach and achieve greatness without the help and wisdom of others in a community. The sense of belonging that high-performance communities cultivate helps us to recognize and believe in our fullest potential. As members of a community, we achieve more because of those around us.

Love can be held together by community. Whether you belong to a professional community or a community of hobbyists, just being around like-minded individuals who share your passion and love for a topic is inspiring. We've all had times when someone asks us a question and our enthusiasm for the subject leads to an hour-long conversation. Embedded in these conversations is a love and joy for the topic and fellowship with someone as excited about it as we are. The affinity and connection built in conversations like this are the main reason we join and maintain membership in communities.

LeBron James and Tom Brady both had teammates who helped them become who they are today. Being in a community of high achievers helps bring out higher achievement for every member.

Confidence and Competence

Confidence and competence are interconnected. Competence, for many of my clients, comes from hiring a coach. They know what they want to accomplish and are clear about their commitment, but they still need a plan for how to proceed. Most aren't confident enough to create one for themselves, so they reach out to someone who can help them design a process that has a guaranteed return on investment and is customized for their needs. When that plan makes sense, confidence increases. With courage, humility, and discipline, they follow the plan. They know they will make mistakes, but also know that they have a coach who can help them make quick course corrections and ensure that they will get better moving forward. Having the plan creates confidence, but full competence is achieved only when that plan is implemented over several months.

QUESTIONS

If greatness is something you want to pursue and achieve personally or want for your employees, you have to train for it today. That requires the traits discussed above. Here are some questions you can ask yourself to determine how ready you are to move toward it.

- What is the idea you love so much that you can't envision it not being achieved?
- When did you reach your point of no return? What did you learn?
- Over the last ninety days, how many times have you and your team experimented and taken risks in service of your customers' experience?
- What one or two leadership behaviors do you perform consistently? Would your team members agree? How do you know?
- Would you describe your team as a community of high performers? Do your customers or most important stakeholders feel the same way?
- What do you need to learn over the next nine to twelve months to close the gap between where you are professionally today and your definition of greatness?

If the questions in Part I have helped you to become clear about what you really love, then you are ready to move on to Part II, where we'll explore how to cultivate the mindset and self-confidence required to pursue your definition of greatness.

PART II

Learn Daily

Introduction to Part II

Part II is targeted for those who have committed to changing the game of work, but recognize that doing so requires that they put their interior lives in order before their exterior lives can be improved. Inside-out change trumps outside-in change and is a courageous act. It takes courage to acknowledge that individual transformation must precede organizational transformation, and to admit that lasting and deep change is best achieved through focus, discipline, and a commitment to exceed our own limits.

Part II is intended to help you pursue a level of personal and professional mastery not experienced before. In it, we'll explore eight traits and characteristics that make the enterprise of living boldly less theoretical and more pragmatic. In order to live boldly, you must conform your life to learning daily about yourself and the subject and object of your love. And by learning daily, I mean just that—not weekly or monthly, but each and every day. Learning daily is the bridge that carries you from loving deeply to living boldly. Learning in service of loving both the people and the work for which you as a leader are responsible is the catalyst for living boldly.

As leaders, we need to learn about a lot of things—the technical aspects of our work, the operational and execution aspects of our enterprises, and the culture, leadership, and team aspects of our employees. All of these are important. But what is often overlooked in the hustle and bustle of organizational life is the need to know yourself and the impact you have on others. How you respond to your operational and leadership challenges has implications for your team and your workplace culture. The more you can build on the upside of this culture and minimize the downside, the more effective a leader you become.

The bottom line? Humble self-knowledge is a more reliable path to living boldly than having volumes of scientific knowledge stored in your brain that you can pull out and showcase at will. Remember, you will not be judged by what you've learned or read, but by how you live your life and the impact you have on others. The next eight chapters discuss the traits and characteristics that serve as the bridge between loving deeply and living boldly.

CHAPTER 7

Humility—Embrace Humble Swagger

Humility is the solid foundation of all virtues.

CONFUCIUS

For all my hard-charging type-A-personality readers, let's start with the good news about humility. Humility does not involve you becoming a wallflower and tolerating poor performance, nor does it require you to become a weak or indecisive leader. Humility doesn't require that you become less confident or passive about achieving your more strategic priorities. And it certainly doesn't require that you put your career aspirations or your professional goals on the back burner.

In his seminal book *The Purpose Driven Life*, Rick Warren tells us: "Humility is not thinking less of yourself, it's thinking of yourself less."[10] You don't have to shrink so that other people can grow. Humility is about being receptive and open to learning from those with whom you work. It's about respecting and trusting them and preserving their personal dignity at all costs. It should be the foundation of all your important relationships, motivating you to ask questions, seek understanding, and work for the greater good of others. In this kind of relationship, you listen curiously and deeply for the insights, wisdom, thoughts, feelings, and beliefs of others. This is the superpower of great leadership.

In his book *Good to Great*, Jim Collins outlined what he called "level-five leadership."[11] In the eleven companies he identified as having gone from good to great, he found that they were all led by the most remarkable CEOs of the century. Yet these remarkable leaders were not common household names. In fact, you have likely never heard of any of them. They were not larger-than-life characters who appeared on the front pages of newspapers or on television talking about their accomplishments. In fact, they were, as Jim Kouzes observed: "ordinary people going about producing extraordinary results."[12]

These leaders teach us an important lesson about humility. Humility isn't passive. These leaders blended humility with a ferocious resolve and an unrelenting determination to build a great company. And this is what I refer to as "humble swagger."

Think back to LeBron James and Tom Brady. Their greatness was built with the double helix of trust and respect—trust that, when they were called on to make the points, they would; and respect for the talent and skill their teammates brought to the team. We often put our sports heroes up on pedestals and forget that their success was the result of a team effort. Tom Brady relied on the offensive line and the receivers on his team. He knew that, when he threw the football to Rob Gronkowski, he would not only catch it, but run farther after the catch than any other receiver on the field. Brady may be called the GOAT, but he wouldn't have achieved the greatness he did without the efforts of his teammates.

My thirty years of watching successful CEOs and entrepreneurs build great companies have convinced me that no one ever achieves their goals by themselves. The loving and bold move—the move that makes you a great leader—is to elevate every employee's skill set and mindset to create uncompromising value for customers. When leaders forget this and no longer want to make a difference in their employees' and customers' lives, it's time for them to make an exit from the ranks of leadership.

When at its very best, humility can create an environment that brings out the best in your team. It unleashes untapped employee potential and converts it into accelerated performance that can lead to a competitive advantage.

BEWARE THE KNOW-IT-ALL

The direct opposite of humility is arrogance, or being a know-it-all. I think we can all agree that no one likes a know-it-all. We respect smart and confident people, but the moment arrogance or "I know best, and you need to listen to me" prevails, performance suffers. When leaders or employees are arrogant and think they have all the answers, underperformance is sure to follow. Teams become overly reliant on the leader making decisions and directing their next steps. Over time, this encourages leaders to over-function and teams to under-function. If neglected long-term, this leads to dysfunctional teams.

Case in point. The worldwide head of human resources of a technology company brought me in to help a brilliant technology CEO who was frustrated with one of his divisional presidents—a financial wonder kid who was intimately involved in every area of his operation. He was a brilliant technologist who rapidly grew his division to $450 million in revenue over three years. But this growth was stalling. Rather than develop new strategies for new markets and looking for ways to eliminate or correct the slowing in his revenue growth, he turned the attention of the CEO to other divisions whose performance lagged behind his. He saw nothing wrong with this and was tone-deaf to the impact he had on others.

My question for the CEO was: "Does this leader want help? Truly want help?" My many years of coaching have led me to agree with the quip often attributed to George Bernard Shaw: "Never wrestle with a pig because you'll both get dirty, and the pig likes it."[13] Coaching someone who doesn't want help is like wrestling a pig. We all choose our behaviors, but some behavior is hard to change. Some of us have become attached to being right, smart, successful, and seen, as in the case of the wonder kid who knew all the answers. The deep change this leader needed to make was not for the timid.

When the CEO broached the subject with his divisional president, he was rebuffed. The employee denied responsibility for the problem and blamed others for the situation. He disregarded a need for openness and receptivity, and refused to see the impact of his behavior on others. He lacked humility and, because of that, lost credibility with the CEO.

Tomas Chamorro-Premuzic asked the key question in a *Forbes* article:

> Why wouldn't we want a humble leader? The answer is that, though we tend to value humility, we are seduced more by other qualities, such as confidence, charisma, and arrogance, that are inversely correlated with humility. When faced with a choice to nominate, select, or elect a leader, humility does not actually feature high on our priority list.[14]

Frank Wagner and Marshall Goldsmith developed a deceptively simple and yet transformational technique called "stakeholder-centered coaching" that addressed this issue.[15]

STAKEHOLDER CENTERED COACHING

Wagner and Goldsmith's technique is grounded in three underlying principles: courage, humility, and discipline. When understood and embraced, this practice has been shown to lead to a 94 percent success rate with coaching clients. Courage and humility are needed to ask for help, listen, and thank stakeholders for their feedback. Both are also needed to reflect on and think about what you are learning about yourself through the process. Courage and discipline are needed to implement suggestions and change your behavior. And most important, discipline is needed to follow up on a regular basis, month after month.

Courage isn't the same thing as fearlessness, however. Fearlessness is the absence of fear, while courage is acting in the presence of fear. Some things scare me that will not scare you, and vice versa. But every endeavor to improve as a leader means we must leave behind what has made us successful in the past and try new behaviors and ways of thinking to achieve new successes. To state the obvious, if you want to accomplish things you've never accomplished before, you have to do things you've never done before. And this takes courage.

As we saw in the careers of Brady and James, humility is about being receptive and open to learning from those with whom you work. It's about respect and trust and personal dignity. It motivates you to ask questions, seek understanding, and work for the greater good of others. And these are powerful tools in the hands of great leaders.

Discipline is the characteristic shared by all great athletes, musicians, artists, and businesspeople. Their excellence is invariably grounded in deep reserves of discipline. They have found what works best for them, and they execute seamlessly and consistently. They recognize that consistency is the key to achieving higher levels of success and deeper levels of satisfaction, and they commit themselves to achieving that consistency through discipline.

QUESTIONS

Here is a mini-survey developed by Frank Wagner and Marshall Goldsmith you can take to determine the level of your courage, your humility, and your discipline. Use it to assess how you are implementing them as you work toward greatness.

Courage

Ask yourself these questions to assess how courageous you are:

- Are you willing to communicate to stakeholders what you want to work on and improve?
- Are you willing to ask them for their feedback and suggestions for improving your behavior?
- Are you willing to avoid procrastination and not wait for a better time to implement new behaviors?
- Are you willing to look at your current behavior honestly and determine what you should stop doing, start doing, or change?

Humility

Use these five questions to determine your level of humility and its impact on those with whom you interact:

- Are you willing to be taught and educated by the people with whom you work and do business?
- Are you willing to ask your stakeholders to help you work on a personal growth goal as a leader?
- Are you willing to listen to feedback and suggestions about your leadership—truly listen?
- Are you willing to show genuine appreciation for feedback and suggestions about your leadership by saying "thank you"?
- Are you willing to keep your ego in check?

Discipline

Ask yourself these five questions to assess how well disciplined you are in your work and your relationships:

- Do you have the discipline to stick with a monthly routine of following up with your stakeholders and asking them for support as you develop your new behaviors?
- Do you have the discipline to manage your defensive reactions while stakeholders point out what you have not done well or what you could do better?
- Are you willing to stop making excuses, getting angry, or disagreeing with feedback that you don't like?
- Are you willing to spend the time needed to change your behavior in ways that aren't comfortable for you?
- Are you willing to spend a few minutes daily reviewing a checklist of actions from a detailed plan to move forward?

As you will see in chapter 8, the humble swagger that can make you an effective leader can be made even more powerful when you adopt the next of the eight characteristics—accountability.

CHAPTER 8

Accountability—Encourage Audacious Accountability

Responsibility equals accountability, accountability equals ownership, and a sense of ownership is the most powerful thing a team or organization can have.

PAT SUMMITT

A web search for the University of Tennessee's women's basketball coach, Pat Summitt, brings up a video of her players speaking about her as a coach. What's powerful in these statements is that her players believe that Pat was much more than a basketball coach. She wasn't concerned just about her players' time on the court; she was also concerned about how they interacted in their communities and with their families. She viewed them as complete individuals with unique lives, not as one-dimensional basketball players. At the time of her retirement, Pat was the winningest women's college basketball coach of all time. Ten years later, she is the second-winningest coach, lagging behind the first-place coach by just one game—and she achieved that in four fewer seasons.

Sometimes it's too easy to draw parallels between sports and boots-on-the-ground leadership and our work lives. But the words of Pat Summit that introduced this chapter can provide important insights into what is necessary for coaching and leading inspired boldness in our own teams. Her emphasis on a sense of ownership as the most powerful thing a team or organization can have points us directly to the fact that accountability sets the tone and culture for the teams or organizations we lead.

All leadership and coaching are relational and interconnected. You can't have success on the basketball court without a coach and a team of players. When coaches work to foster interconnectedness with humility, a bond of trust and respect is created that is impervious to adversity and setbacks. Without that trust and respect, opportunities are missed and potential goes unrealized. And without accountability, trust and respect have a hard time thriving.

RESISTING ACCOUNTABILITY

There are six key reasons why we are sometimes so resistant to holding ourselves accountable for our actions: we have a hard time seeing ourselves clearly; we don't like to admit it when our behavior has hurt or damaged others; we sometimes find it difficult to own the behaviors we choose; we avoid setting and articulating high personal standards; we find it easy to defend ourselves when our own standards go unmet; and we often lack the brutal honesty with ourselves and others that is required to effect positive change. Let's look more closely at each of these obstacles and try to understand how overcoming them can lead to greater personal and professional accountability.

Seeing Ourselves Clearly

It's hard to see ourselves clearly. We all have some idea of the type of person we are or that we want to be. We have an image in our mind's eye, and we believe there's alignment between what we aspire to do and what we actually do. We give ourselves wide latitude in our behavior because we believe that what we aspire to achieve or become is noble and uplifting for us.

But we have a high capacity to deceive ourselves about our effectiveness in achieving our ideals. We are sometimes anesthetized by the reality of the situation around us and need an outsider who can act as our go-to truth-teller. Unfortunately, we rely too often on our internal resources, where the level of trust, respect, and candor is lower. We all need someone we trust and respect to help us see our current reality in ways we cannot see ourselves. Only with this clarity can we be truly accountable.

Avoiding Blame

We all have a tendency to confuse our intentions with our impact. Most of us work and lead with positive intent. We want to do good, to make a difference. We want to do our very best. But too often our intentions don't align with the impact we have on others and on situations. We may say something or do something that negatively impacts others or confuses them. And when we learn this has happened, we believe that people should give us the benefit of the doubt and somehow judge us by our intentions rather than our impact. We secretly hope that we won't be held to a high standard.

But this kind of denial leads us to belittle our own potential and set lower standards for ourselves. And when you are not giving your best to others, you shouldn't expect them to give their best to you.

Owning Our Behavior

There's no way to avoid the fact that our behavior does one of two things: it either lifts people up, or it tears them down. It provides encouragement, hope, and faith in what is possible, or removes them. I think we can all agree on an intellectual level that we should take ownership for the behaviors we choose. But in the crucible of hard facts, it can be humbling and disorienting to acknowledge how our behavior has negatively impacted others. By being accountable for those behaviors, we encourage an attitude of trust in those around us. And this helps pave the way to greatness.

Setting High Standards

The standards we set for others in environments where trust and respect are low are typically higher than those we set for ourselves. This is rooted in an us-versus-them attitude.

In my coaching and leadership work, I infrequently see leaders who intentionally and purposely set higher standards for others than they set for themselves. What I do find, however, is that the standards people set for themselves are frequently lower than what they're capable of meeting. When we hold ourselves to the highest standards—and by that, I mean the standards that promote greatness and inspire boldness—we welcome being held accountable for them, because this communicates to others how we will do business.

Making Excuses

When we defend ourselves or deny falling short of the standards we have set for ourselves, we say "no" to the feedback we're getting, perhaps making excuses and saying that we couldn't meet the standard because of being tired or overscheduled, or for some other reason. Or worse, we may even deflect constructive criticism by pointing a finger at the person giving it and telling them they weren't clear in the first place and are therefore to blame. This not only destroys our credibility. It undermines the trust and respect without which greatness can not be achieved.

Brutal Honesty

It's hard to be brutally honest with ourselves and others. It takes courage. Can you tell yourself the unvarnished truth about what people experience when they interact with you? You will likely say "yes." But it can be hard for us to change our behavior regarding important issues, and the same holds true with regard to holding ourselves accountable.

Nonetheless, we can, in fact, all choose different behaviors when confronted with the uncomfortable truth that our behavior isn't serving the people who matter most to us. Remember: humility underpins the ability to be accountable. Not being arrogant, being open and receptive, and not trying to be the smartest person in the room enables a greater amount of responsibility, accountability, and, as Pat Summitt said, ownership.

A key truth about accountability is that leaders go first taking responsibility. They don't wait for their teams to take the plunge. They are proactive, and, as I said in the title of this chapter, audacious in accepting accountability. They don't deny or blame or deflect, because leaders who have fallen in love with an idea, a hope, a dream, or an aspiration take ownership first. If you aspire to greatness, accountability is a must-have trait. It results when leaders set high standards and inspire their teams to passionately pursue meeting those standards.

QUESTIONS

Here are some questions you can ask yourself to determine whether you are being truly accountable in your leadership:

- How often do you have a conversation with your leadership team—or your spouse or significant other—about how well you are living up to the values that you hold to be most important? What might you learn from these conversations?

- Can you identify five high standards that you have set for yourself? If you shared your list with someone you

trust and respect and asked them how closely your behavior aligns with your standards, what might they say?

- Based on the answers to these questions, identify five
behaviors you will share with your team and ask that
they hold you accountable for them.

In the next chapter, we'll explore empowerment and the importance of dreaming big dreams.

CHAPTER 9

Empowerment—Dream Bigger Dreams

If you don't like the road you're walking, start paving another one.

DOLLY PARTON

In 1998, I decided to sell my financial-services business and enter the consulting and coaching field. I didn't have a clear idea of how I would do this, but I was certain it would entail, as Dolly Parton suggested, "paving another road." I was passionate about leadership, communication, and teams. I had a shelf full of books on the subjects, and I'd been working with coaches in athletics for over three decades. I had a conviction that I could help teams and leaders convert human potential into inspired performance. I had a problem, however. I had no connections in the consulting world and didn't know anyone in the field. To be attractive to a company, I needed to build my skills in the real world. But to do that, I needed to have experience in the real world.

One thing I did know, however, was the importance of empowerment. I knew that I could empower others by sharing my insights, my wisdom, and my experiences. And I knew that I could empower myself by being proactive and paving my own path forward in pursuit of my hopes and dreams, as opposed to waiting for those dreams to drop into my lap. So I chose to do both. I went on a two-month journey to build relationships in my new field. I committed to having coffee with two people every day to learn what was important to them. I committed to sharing one idea I thought could be helpful, and to learning where the opportunities were in the field. By week seven, I knew I was building great connections, but I felt no farther down the road to finding where my own next opportunity lay. I was losing my confidence.

Then I met Nancy, who had heard of me from one of my new connections. She listened to me tell my story, found my desire to make a difference compelling, and said she would introduce me to Dick Heller, VP and Chief Inspiration Officer for the Tom Peters Company, whose founder was the author of *In Search of Excellence*.[16]

Nancy was empowering me to take the next step in my professional journey by introducing me to an expert in the field. When I met him in California, Dick was cordial and engaging, and asked lots of good questions. At the end of forty-five minutes, he invited me to send him a demo video of myself facilitating a group. Needless to say, I was thrilled and excited about the possibility of breaking into the field.

Well, I didn't just record a video. I produced a presentation of such high quality that Dick Heller, a former producer for public television in Boston, admired it. I created a video that was different from what anyone else would have done, because I was determined to give myself the best possible shot at fulfilling my dream. Dick called two weeks later and said it was quite good. Then he invited me to join the Tom Peters Company.

That was in 2000. Over the last twenty-three years, I have worked on three continents, in seven countries, and in forty-five states. I have traveled the world and had the privilege and honor of working with world-renowned enterprises to convert human potential into inspired performance. My big dream paid off.

FIVE KEYS TO EMPOWERMENT

Dick had a gift when it came to developing people and I learned a lot from him about empowerment. I was thrust onto the front lines with him as he empowered me to use my natural talents and skills in the service of his company's intellectual property and to provide high value to their clients.

Dick taught me that there are five keys to empowerment: autonomy, clarity, competence, mentorship, and high standards. When these five elements are in place, the path to success becomes smoother. Let's look at each one to determine just how they contribute to the achievement of greatness.

Autonomy

Dick was someone who believed in giving people autonomy over their own talents and authority over their own learning. He gave me the freedom to take on a body of work and chunk it down in ways that made sense for me. He trusted me to learn about it, integrate it, and teach it. He granted me ownership over my own learning and growth by mapping out a clear path of development for me that linked my business objectives with my professional goals. He was not a micromanager, nor did he try to control each and every step of my development. And this empowered me to move forward in pursuit of my dream.

Clarity

Dick was a great listener. As someone coming into the field flat-footed and without a lot of experience, I had lots of questions and fears and reservations. He knew and accepted that. When I expressed concerns or doubts, he never lost his patience. He never dismissed my fears or diminished them. He just listened to them without judgment. When I wasn't clear about what steps to take next, he clarified things. He tied everything I was doing to the larger picture of the organization's goals. He made sure I understood how my efforts would contribute to the overall success of the company, and provided regular feedback that was rich with deep insights from his thirty years in the field. This empowered me to overcome my doubts and clarify my goals.

Competence

When it came to building my skills and getting up to speed quickly, Dick remained clear and focused as to what I needed to learn next. He had me take small chunks of content and deliver it to people throughout the company, as well as in my personal life. He provided me with a coach and a mentor who helped identify my talents and skills, and determine how they could best be utilized in service of doing what was right for a client. This empowered me to refine those skills and find ways to apply them in pursuit of my goals.

Mentorship

Dick provided me with a creative and supportive environment. Most everyone with whom I worked was a seasoned professional. I was the only person who didn't have any facilitation or corporate experience. But he positioned me within the rest of the organization as an asset in the fields of financial services and healthcare, and designed ways for me to partner with other consultants in those domains. I had insights that I could bring to bear from an operational and strategic perspective. In the process of sharing those insights, I learned how to do the coaching and consulting work I love. This mentorship empowered me to place a high value not only on where I wanted to go, but also on where I had been.

High Standards

Dick set high standards for me, even though I was an inexperienced rookie. There were no free passes. He held me accountable to a clear set of standards and never deviated from them. He made sure I knew what was at stake for the clients, for the salespeople, and for myself. He helped me understand the impact of my decisions and actions on the rest of the team, giving me ownership of small things at first, but eventually giving me the opportunity to lead projects. He convinced me that greatness was possible and, through all these ways, empowered me to pursue it.

Autonomy, clarity, competence, mentorship, and high standards are components of empowerment that all leaders can bring to their teams. The autonomy to experiment and take risks is very much a part of empowerment. Clarifying goals leads to competence, while mentoring and high standards inspire superior performance. I also learned that micromanagement is rarely productive, and that trust and respect are critical factors in leadership. It was this kind of empowerment that encouraged me and inspired me to become a world-class coach and consultant.

QUESTIONS

Ask yourself these five questions to discover whether you are successfully empowering others or yourself:

- When you think of the person who had the most impact on your commitment to empowering your team, what specifically did they do, and how do you rate yourself compared to their example?
- On a scale of one to ten, what rating would you give your leadership team for bringing out the best in their teams?
- What talent or skill do you and your leadership team need to develop to be considered exemplars of transformational and empowered cultures?
- In thinking about the people you are currently mentoring or coaching, what are the three to five issues with which they need the most help? On a scale of one to ten, how successful have you been in helping them?

- How have you raised the standards to which you hold yourself accountable in your leadership coaching or mentoring?

Humility, accountability, and empowerment are all noble and uplifting objectives. But unless you cultivate passion in your everyday affairs, you may find it difficult to cultivate it in your larger goals. We'll look at that in the next chapter.

CHAPTER 10

Passion—Cultivate the Will to Win

The will to win, the desire to succeed, the urge to reach your full potential . . . these are the keys that will unlock the door to personal excellence.

CONFUCIUS

As we have seen, there is a direct link between knowing what you really want and achieving greatness. To achieve greatness, you must have the will to win and the desire to succeed and reach your full potential. But you also have to know what winning means in the context of what you love. Otherwise, you will feel little desire to embrace learning daily. In fact, you have to put your desires under the microscope in order to fully understand what winning or losing means to you. What do succeeding or failing mean to you? How will you know whether you are achieving your full potential or avoiding it?

Tom Brady and LeBron James shared a desire to be the very best at their respective sports, and that desire was so compelling that they organized their lives around it. They both had coaches and were continually looking for an edge—no matter how small. They were both committed to learning something today that would make them better players tomorrow. That may have made them hard to live with. It takes someone very special to love and support a type-A, hard-charging, excellence-pursuing athlete. Their professional lives can be cut short in one game; they are constantly faced with the possibility that today could be their last game. But that knowledge just pushes them to achieve their definition of excellence as soon as possible, because there is no guaranteed tomorrow.

FIRE IN THE BELLY

People who don't have the same fire in the belly for winning don't feel the same level of urgency for action as excellence-minded athletes and leaders. Excellence-minded individuals have a narrow scope of priorities and see time as limited and precious. They limit their deepest desires and focus an inordinate amount of attention on a few critically important goals.

Most of us have a lot of desires. We may want to live in a bigger home or own a new car. We may want to weigh fifteen pounds less or have more rewarding professional and personal relationships. We may want to be respected by our peers or professional community. We may even want to change the world. But our deepest desire, the one built into every human being, is the desire to be loved—by our families, our friends, our communities, or our teams. This is our most fundamental desire, and the further we move away from it or deny it, the more apt we are to replace it with other lesser desires that we hope will fill the hole of not feeling loved.

This last paragraph is not intended as an existential or philosophical sidebar. It is meant to explain why questioning our desires, both personally and professionally, is important.

Take a few seconds to answer three short questions about your desires.

- How do you define winning at home and at work? Using your definition, give yourself a score of one to ten for both your home and work definition.
- How do you define success? While this may seem similar to winning, give it a shot. Then rate yourself again on a scale of one to ten.
- What does your full potential look like? Define that, then rate yourself using the same scale.

Now, look at your answers. Do you like what you see, or are you concerned? Are there dreams, hopes, and aspirations in each answer? Have you settled for something less in any way? Have you tamed your desire to win based on unfulfilled goals? Or do you just want a higher score?

If you really want to learn more about how you see your own success and whether you are reaching your full potential, share your responses with your spouse, or partner, or significant other. Ask them to answer the questions for themselves first; then ask them to answer the questions based on how they think *you* answered them. Finally, compare your answers. The insights you gain from this exercise will give greater impact to the topics discussed in the rest of this chapter.

PASSIONATE DESIRES

Over the last three and a half years of a worldwide pandemic, many people have tamed their professional desires and stopped dreaming of a better future. A recent Kaiser Family Foundation report states that 90 percent of Americans believe the country is facing a mental-health crisis. "The pandemic has affected the public's mental health and well-being in a variety of ways," it claims, "including through isolation and loneliness, job loss and financial instability, and illness and grief."[17]

This study's conclusions are reenforced by a significant spike in mental-health, alcohol, and drug-related insurance claims. In fact, the National Institutes of Health found that, in 2021, nearly half of Americans surveyed reported recent symptoms of an anxiety or depressive disorder, and 10 percent of respondents felt their mental-health needs were not being met.[18] Moreover, the study found that rates of anxiety, depression, and substance-use disorders increased over the course of the pandemic. Add to this the brain-, heart-, and soul-numbing prospect of resuming three-hour daily commutes and you have a true cultural crisis. These factors have led many to decide to put their deepest desires on the back burner in the belief that thriving is a pipe dream and survival is all that's possible.

In hundreds of interviews with teams over the past eighteen months, I have heard a persistent and troubling refrain—that giving up on big dreams was the safest path forward, and that their needs were best served by focusing on much smaller and achievable desires. These smaller desires could be fulfilled easily, while bigger dreams were uncertain and harder to achieve. These individuals had become anesthetized to what was possible and were settling for what was acceptable. They were grazing on the cotton candy of pedestrian desires as opposed to feasting on a nutrient-dense menu of excellence desires. They had hit the brakes on their dreams and given up the will to win. And many of them were customer-facing.

This raises a number of key questions: Does your team have one fully named and fully designed desire that it is ready to act upon? Have you articulated an insatiable hunger to do something your customers or stakeholders have deemed worthy of the term "excellent"? Or have you simply expressed an intellectual curiosity about some project, but not approached it with passion? Are your employees experiencing any of the negative mental-health effects or anxieties brought on by the pandemic? If so, how has this influenced the way they define the customer experience—or the employee experience, for that matter? Is excellence embedded into every aspect of the employee and customer experience?

Don't get me wrong, excellence looks different in every industry. But it always requires asking what you and your team are hungry for professionally. What would excellence look like in your most important strategic priority? What does it look like to your customers? Do any of your answers excite you?

"The purpose of business is to create a customer," Peter Drucker points out.[19] And as we learned in Part I, when you love your customers, you design and organize your whole operation around their satisfaction. Every aspect of your interactions with them is choreographed to delight them and lead them to describe you as a great business partner.

GREATNESS IS HARD

Mediocrity is easy, but greatness is hard work, even when espoused by the highest echelons of leadership. There are no shortcuts to greatness. If you're looking for a hack or some sort of easy path to greatness, you absolutely will not find one in this book. Every single chapter here requires that you give something of yourself. Each chapter pushes you to ask yourself deeper questions than you've likely asked yourself before. Each chapter asks you to infuse love into every nook and cranny of your business, and see how transformative that four-letter word can be.

When you infuse passion into your work, you ensure that, when you ask for more, you receive more. When your mindset is passionately committed to the pursuit of greatness, everything changes. You will likely be startled into a new way of thinking—a way of thinking "bigger." And when you think bigger, when you have bolder goals, you become dissatisfied with just being good and aspire to greatness. You lead people toward a destination that fulfills your customers', your employees', and your organizations' deepest desires.

"Be a yardstick of quality," Steve Jobs advised. Some people aren't used to an environment where greatness is expected, because their leaders have become anesthetized to bold dreams. They don't act as role models for greatness; they act as advocates for mediocrity. Leaders have to fight hard against accepting average results or mediocrity. They must articulate a clear, compelling, and bold goal and paint a mental picture of what the situation will look like three years in the future. Their enthusiasm and exuberance for boldness and greatness must be contagious. Does that describe you? Are you modeling the humility and accountability and empowerment required to achieve greatness?

Remember: When you pursue greatness, you can't blame others or deny the current situation if you don't achieve it. You have to care deeply about it and own the outcomes where adjustments need to be made. And you can't micromanage and try to fix everything. You have to leave people free to experiment and empower them to take risks. There are no control freaks in the pursuit of greatness.

As you will see, the next chapter plays a vital role in helping you to implement each of the four characteristics you've learned about so far—humility, accountability, empowerment, and passion. All these traits and characteristics are fractal. By that, I mean that, within each one, you will find elements of all the other traits and characteristics. They're not independent from one another; they're *interdependent*—woven together with the invisible thread of desires and actions that can help pave your road to greatness.

QUESTIONS

As you consider whether or not you are passionately committed to the path of greatness, ask yourself these questions:

- Can you provide testimonials that showcase your capacity for providing a great business advantage to your customers?
- When you go two levels down in your organization, can 80 percent of your employees articulate your strategy for customer greatness and their role in accomplishing it with clarity and confidence—in sixty seconds or less?
- Do you have replicable processes in place for accomplishing high-value work, reducing costs, and delighting your customers?
- When you look throughout your department, are employees continually and willingly raising the bar on their own performance without prompts from management?
- Is the prevailing mindset in your department one of experimentation, risk-taking, and growth?
- When you last brainstormed with your team, how many times in the previous two weeks had they had a great customer experience? What made it great? What can you and they learn from that? How do your customers answer that same question about your team or company?

If you stopped reading here and devoted yourself to embodying these first four characteristics, you would be a better leader and coach. You might even be really good. Now let's move on from the *what* of greatness to the *how* of it. And that brings us to the all-important characteristic of a dedication to knowledge—what I call "Formula One learning."

CHAPTER 11

Formula One Learning— Accelerate Growth

An investment in knowledge pays the best interest.

BEN FRANKLIN

In what was one of the most intense and thrilling moments in my life, I found myself doing 147 miles per hour at the Porsche racing school in what is best described as a rocket ship built on four wheels. The engine, only a few inches from my head, pounded in my chest as if I were receiving CPR, and the trees flew by so fast that they were no longer trees, but more a blurry green swatch of color that I saw out of the corner of my eye.

I had gone there to learn how to drive fast. Not to race down main street from one traffic light to the next, but to become a more educated and safer driver in all types of circumstances. Learning the subtle nuances of when and how to shift gears, when to accelerate and when to brake, I left with a vastly improved lap time, as well as a greatly enhanced mindset behind the wheel.

I am not a professional driver, nor do I race cars regularly. I am an enthusiast. I'm someone who loves racing—particularly Formula One racing. It's a wickedly expensive sport. There are only ten teams, each with up to 1200 employees, seventy-five of whom travel to the track on race day. Just as in the organization for which you work, there are leaders in every area of the operation—general managers, team principles, technical directors, data engineers, strategists, head mechanics, lead mechanics for each area of the car, and, of course, drivers. The drivers are the ones who put their lives on the line and take ownership for pushing the $15 million four-wheeled rocket to its very limits.

Many of my high-performance coaching clients feel as if they are on the track, racing to accomplish their priorities. They don't have time for pit stops or taking a deep breath. They don't take time to discern whether what they're doing is producing the best results possible. They're driving fast, but learning slowly.

So how can you create a learning culture where you learn as fast as a Formula One racing team travels? I've found three key strategies that can accelerate learning and growth: slow down, seek wisdom, and put people first. Let's look at each one to see how they can accelerate your journey down the road to greatness.

SLOW DOWN

This may seem counterintuitive, but it's true. To go fast, you have to slow down. In Formula One racing and other professional sports, first-year drivers and players share a common experience when they enter their second year. They report that the race or game slows down appreciably and that this allows them to see things that were hidden to them previously. They begin to feel as if they're not simply keeping up, but are now playing and driving up to their potential.

We live in a noisy world. The sounds of our electronics are ubiquitous. Our radios or TVs are always on and our minds never turn off. As Anna Lembke observes in her book *Dopamine Nation*:

> We're living in a time of unprecedented access to high-reward, high-dopamine stimuli: drugs, food, news, gambling, shopping, gaming, texting, sexting . . . The increased numbers, variety, and potency is staggering. The smartphone is the modern-day hypodermic needle, delivering digital dopamine 24/7 for a wired generation. As such we've all become vulnerable to compulsive overconsumption.[20]

This overconsumption has a debilitating impact on our leadership and our ability to focus, to get into flow, and, yes, to lead boldly.

When we are in information overload, we tend to skim the surface of our most important priorities and make decisions that simply allow us to check one more thing off our to-do list, then move on to our next most urgent issue. Thanks to our noisy world, we have become incapable of asking deeper questions and gleaning new insights about how to live or lead boldly. We are on the fast track in life with our foot glued to the accelerator, pedal to the metal.

The first step toward liberating ourselves from the tyranny of these distractions is a truly revolutionary act. It's so countercultural that, when you try this for the first time, you may experience withdrawal symptoms. Once a week for a month, I have each of my clients schedule a one- to two-hour meeting that is totally "unplugged." That means no phone, no email, no online interactions, no texts, nothing. Zero. Zilch. Nada.

The benefit? One client said it best: "This one two-hour window allows me to accomplish a week's worth of strategically important work in one session." How many people in your organization accomplish a week's worth of strategically important work in one two-hour window? What if there were two sessions? What if there were one for each of your leadership teams?

Creating the structure and discipline to do this work is similar to what goes into training and structuring a Formula One team. It takes endurance, coordination, and focus—all things that are in short supply in today's corporate world. But with endurance, coordination, and focus, you can create the systems and structure required to empower employees to work a "one-day month"—a one-day sprint in which the most strategic priority for a month is accomplished in one day. That's the power of slowing down.

SEEK WISDOM

Once you've unplugged yourself (and others) from the drug of information, you can turn your attention to seeking wisdom—first about yourself, and then about your teams. As a leader, the only tool you have in your tool kit is yourself. So when you set out to seek the wisdom you need to be a great leader, look first to yourself and the impact you are having on others and on your teams. The wisdom necessary to lead boldly requires that you have the humility to ask for help, the accountability to listen and take ownership of what you learn, the empowerment that allows others to tell you the truth, and a clearly articulated idea of what winning looks like for you and your teams.

A client of mine who is a vice president in the education field asks me one question without fail at the end of every call: "Based on today's call, what two suggestions can you give me that will help me be a better leader?" She is a heat-seeking missile for feedback and feed-forward for how to get better. This places her in the top 2 percent of those clients who grow the most.

Another of her wisdom-seeking best practices is setting clear intentions for each day. She sets her intentions first thing in the morning and never has more than three. She writes them on a piece of paper with a brief explanation of why they're important. At the end of the day, she writes down answers to the following questions:

- How did I do in fulfilling my intentions?
- What can I learn about my leadership, my team, and my impact?
- What is one thing I can do differently tomorrow to be more effective than I was today?

This isn't rocket science, nor does it require the same level of infrastructure as a Formula One racing team. But this consistent daily practice has accelerated her growth exponentially. Yes, she has a dream for the department she loves. She loves her team members and wants to help them flourish at work. But first she puts herself under the microscope and takes responsibility for her learning.

This process slows her down. And that's a good thing. It takes less than five minutes daily to see things that she didn't see the day before, which allows her to be just a little bit better the next day.

PUT PEOPLE FIRST

In his first book *In Search of Excellence,* Tom Peters presented this novel idea: "The magic formula that successful businesses have discovered is to treat customers like guests and employees like people."[21] Forty-one years later, Peters is advocating for another idea that he calls "extreme humanism," encouraging businesses to put their people first:

> It's my conclusion that . . . putting people first and helping them prepare for a rocky future, vigorously and passionately supporting our communities, providing products and services that stun our clientele with their excellence and verve, serving our ailing planet, is, perhaps counterintuitively, the best path forward.[22]

Alan Mulally advises the same in his "Working Together" system, where he claims that his success was rooted in building teams that understood and adhered to one simple principle: "People come first . . . Love them up."[23]

Do you love your people up? Do you build on their strengths and capitalize on their experience? Do you respect their opinions and empower them to do their best work? Are you willing to give up some of your control and give them free rein to experiment and take risks? Do you practice the principles outlined in the last four chapters?

I believe and trust that most leaders and readers do put people first, but all too often that happens only when things are going well. When the yogurt hits the fan and your company misses Wall Street's expectations, what happens then? Do people come first? Or do profits come first?

One airline CEO was once told on a quarterly investor call that he was spending too much on employee benefits. His response: "Sell your stock." He used some other words that were a little racy as well, but the bottom line was that anyone who didn't like the fact that he and his team treated customers like guests and employees like people should find another place to invest their money.

How do you go about loving your employees? You implement what you learned in the last four chapters. It's not rocket science, nor does it require a lot of preparation and help from the employee-relations department. Just ask them what they think. Ask rather than making statements, and listen to understand rather than responding, as Stephen Covey recommended. Here are some questions that can get the ball rolling:

- What is it that I need to learn as team leader to help this team be successful moving forward?
- As team leader, was there anything I missed or didn't listen to that would have made the situation better?
- What strengths do we have that were not fully implemented?
- What weaknesses inhibit our success?

- Did we take any shortcuts that damaged our results?
- Did we do the right thing, but do it incorrectly? Or did we do the wrong thing, but do it correctly?
- What are the top five lessons we've learned from this situation?
- What are two or three ways that we can convert the negatives of this situation into positives?
- Did we pursue excellence and miss the mark? Or did we engage in poor planning and preparation?

FAIL FORWARD FASTER

Whenever you aim high or pursue greatness, there will be times when you fail or don't achieve your desired results. What happens in these moments is crucial, not only for the future of your team's performance, but for the quality of your relationships with your team and your customers.

I once worked with an accounting firm where I asked the managing partner how he approached failure and what mechanisms he had in place for improving the systems and processes in his firm. He looked at me with complete sincerity and said: "Well, we are an advanced CPA firm, and yes, we tolerate failure. Just as long as there aren't any negative consequences." When I asked how he defined negative consequences, he replied: "Oh, that's easy. We don't lose money, a client, our reputation, efficiency, or productivity."

In healthy cultures with bold leaders, there's a generosity surrounding failure—not a tolerance for poor planning and carelessness, but a generosity when team members willingly and voluntarily raise the bar on their performance and fall short. Healthy cultures embrace learning from mistakes, while erecting barriers to keep from making the same mistake twice. In your organization, is failure tolerated? Is it celebrated? Does it matter if it's done with the right motivations? Or is failure punished?

You can't pursue excellence without making mistakes. It's not uncommon to get worse before getting better. We'll look more closely at how to manage the inevitable mistakes that occur in the pursuit of greatness in chapter 20, where we'll talk about something called the Stretch 100 Project.

QUESTIONS

Take some time to examine how your enterprise encourages wisdom and responds to situations in which outcomes fall short of stated goals.

- How many times over the last ninety days have you and your leadership team had a one- to two-hour deep-focus-and-flow session without any interruptions? What's the impact of your answer?
- The average knowledge worker gets interrupted fifty-six times per day. What strategies have you implemented to reduce these interruptions or to help employees recover faster?
- How many referrals for new employees have you received from other employees in the last six months?
- Do employees feel safe experimenting, taking risks, and making mistakes in your organization, or are they afraid to do so?
- In the last three months, what have you learned about your leadership that has prompted you to set a stretch goal for your leadership growth?

I cannot emphasize enough that, if you want to accelerate learning in your organization, it has to start with you. If you are not role-modeling and embracing learning about your leadership and its impact, this shows your employees that, although you embrace the idea of learning as an intellectual construct, you're not living it. If this is true for you, the next chapter will hold some important insights for you about a pivotal and powerful leadership trait—integrity.

CHAPTER 12

Integrity—Keep Your Word

In looking for people to hire, look for three things: integrity, intelligence, and energy. If they don't have the first, the other two will kill you.

WARREN BUFFET

In the 1950s, Edward R. Murrow was known and respected as a broadcast journalist and war correspondent who came into prominence during World War II by recruiting a team of reporters who brought the realities of fighting on the front lines to life. They were eventually known as the Murrow Boys. Murrow was a pioneer in radio and television, and was considered by many to be one of journalism's greatest figures.

Murrow hosted a broadcast named *This I Believe,* on which ordinary men and women—bankers, butchers, actors, and celebrities—shared what they believed and how they lived their lives. Although they came from very different walks of life, they all had one thing in common: a set of values or beliefs that guided their lives. In the opening of the first show, Murrow stated that the only things required for people to be on the show were integrity, honesty, and the ability to discuss the rules by which they live. This show became a model for helping listeners understand the values and virtues of everyday people, and reducing the fear, uncertainty, and doubt some felt about their fellow Americans. After a four-year run, the show was canceled. Fifty years later, it was relaunched in a similar format, but focusing on notable individuals—celebrities, athletes, and other high-profile people.

In 2009, Muhammad Ali gave a compelling interview that was delivered by his wife, because his Parkinson's disease had taken a toll on his ability to communicate. In it, the world heavyweight boxing champion and Olympic gold medalist talked about his boycott of the Vietnam War, his conversion to the Nation of Islam, his philanthropic activities, and his fight for social justice.

What was most striking about this episode was Ali's supreme self-confidence. His parents, he claimed, had raised him to believe in himself and never to doubt what he was capable of doing. He *knew* that he was going to be the heavyweight boxing champion of the world, and that he would go on to win an Olympic gold medal. Ali was clear about what he believed and what he wanted. He knew what greatness looked like for him and held himself 100 percent accountable for his training, embracing learning and getting better every day. He sought wisdom from others and went through life with unprecedented swagger, although with regard to his faith, he was a humble man. Ali exemplified many of the leadership traits we're discussing here. And they all worked together to help him achieve greatness. But perhaps more than anything else, he was known for his integrity.

THE INTEGRITY PROBLEM

If you were asked if you wanted to be known as a person of integrity, I believe that most of us would answer in the affirmative without hesitation. If the question were changed to whether you are *currently* a person of integrity, you would probably also answer in the affirmative. But if asked whether the people who matter most to you at work and at home *describe* you as a person of integrity, you might hesitate before answering, because, although you hope they would, you don't know for sure. The problem is that, while we all tend to judge our own integrity through the prism of our intent, others judge our integrity through the prism of our actions.

Unless you are crystal clear about the traits or beliefs that guide and animate your life, it's difficult at best to live an authentic and aligned life that causes others to see you as a person of integrity. The clearer you are about what's most important to you and why, the better able you will be to have the kind of impact on others that turbocharges your leadership abilities. When you act from integrity, it removes all the doubt that employees, partners, or stakeholders may have about what you value and what you expect of them.

People today are tired, confused, and battered by the cultural malaise in which we're living. The fears and divisions that have reshaped our public discourse have led to an unprecedented degree of hopelessness and disengagement at work and in our communities at large. What people want is someone who has character, is confident, and has charisma. When you are clear about what you believe and why, and are unafraid to act upon it, people begin to see these qualities in you and look upon you as a leader. This clarity isn't a "nice-to-have" quality in today's world of work. It's a "must-have" quality.

PROJECTING INTEGRITY

Imagine you've been contacted for an interview on *This I Believe*. They want to interview you—live—about what you believe and how you live your life. Would you agree to the interview? This may seem like a ridiculous scenario to you, but in fact, it happens to you every day. You may not be interviewed on the air, but you are "interviewed" every day by your employees and stakeholders for the job of being a person worthy of their trust. And your responses determine whether you did what you said you would do to make their lives better.

A colleague of mine who is a communication consultant shared a framework for preparing for a meeting or interview that projects your integrity to others. It consists of five questions you can ask yourself that, when answered authentically and honestly, can help convince others of your integrity.

- What is it I want people to think?
- What is it I want people to feel?
- What is it I want people to know?
- What is it I want people to believe?
- What is it I want people to do to move forward or to engage?

Let's look at each one of these questions separately and consider their possible outcomes.

Thinking

Consider your audience and ask yourself what they are currently thinking. Then ask yourself about their experience and what questions they may be asking themselves. The answers to these questions may help you determine if there are mental frameworks, metaphors, or ideas they work within that you need to know about, to address, or to change. Know your audience before moving to the second question.

Feeling

It's important to remember that people make decisions emotionally and justify them logically. Are there feelings in the room of which you need to be aware? After your interview or meeting, what do you want people to feel? Use the words you want people to experience, but do so with sincerity. You cannot fake sincerity.

Knowing

What are the facts you want people to know or can share with them about yourself or a project? Consider things they need to know about the process, the outcomes, the people involved, the challenges, and the rewards. This will make it easier to convince them that you'll work to make your project as rewarding an experience as possible.

Believing

What do you want your audience to believe? This is similar to, but different from, what they know. Knowing is about facts and data, while believing is about conviction and agreement. Consider how you can build the credibility and belief

in who you are and what you believe so that your target
audience will be convinced of your integrity.

Doing
This question is the call to action for you and your listeners.
It's the simple "here's what we need to do next" part of the
conversation. If you have been honest about how you asked
the previous four questions, and thoughtful about what the
answers to those questions mean to your goals, your audience will be ready to trust in your integrity and move forward with you down the path to success.

All these questions about integrity are interconnected with
the other traits we've been exploring. Humility is about listening and not having all the answers. Accountability is about
not blaming or denying the current situation. Empowerment
speaks to the need for experimenting and taking risks. The
clear articulation of bold goals helps others know what you
believe and why. And learning cultivates the growth necessary to move forward by working together.

In the world of work, when you do what you say you will
do, the trust and confidence people have in you go up. When
you do what you say you will do, you gain credibility and
that increases your influence. And that influence is essential
when your definition of greatness is bold and requires adopting new ways of working.

QUESTIONS

Here is a simple self-assessment practice that can help you
increase the likelihood that others will see you as a person
of integrity.

- Use your phone to record a two- to three-minute interview about what you believe and share it with someone you trust and respect. What feedback do you get?
- Based on your recording (or writing), for what do you want to be known? For what traits do you want your stakeholders to hold you accountable?
- What two or three traits that we've covered so far bring out your very best?
- Ask your direct reports what three or four non-negotiables you hold to be most important. Are they accurate?
- What percent of the time do you keep your commitments, and what percent of the time do you break them?

These are not navel-gazing philosophical questions. They are foundational questions whose answers speak to your believability and whether teams are willing to follow your lead.

If what you believe resonates with others, you have positive influence. If what you believe is self-serving and focused solely on the tasks or work, you will not win the hearts and minds of those you lead. If you want to pursue greatness boldly, you have to believe in elevated human potential. Your job as leader is to find that potential and bring it out. And that's what we'll talk about in the next chapter.

CHAPTER 13

Collaboration—Make Teammates Better

The most important measure of how good a game I played was how much better I'd made my teammates play.

BILL RUSSELL, NBA LEGEND

Louisa is a highly capable leader who has been promoted three times in six years because of her ability to get excellent results while building high-performance teams. She believes that being smart and talented is only one part of success at work. Success at work also requires relationships in which people collaborate to create something bigger than what one person alone can create. Louisa believes deeply in the saying: "If you want to go fast, go alone. If you want to go far, go together."

One day, I got a request from Louisa to help her assess an employee named David, a technology whiz kid who, while telegraphing the message of "Let's go together," did everything to make others want to go it alone without him. Louisa characterized him as someone who walks a razor-thin line between being someone you trust and could see as a good friend, and someone you want sentenced to life in prison. My head spun as I sat in the conference room listening to him discuss strategic priorities for mergers and acquisitions:

> Our acquisition of . . . was made ten years ago. In the first three years, we worked to integrate their employees into our culture and their technology onto our platform. We have not been successful in doing so. Their culture was entrepreneurial and nimble, and ours is the opposite. We work in silos, and they work in collaborative teams. They talk to their customers, and we say we do, but we don't really. Their employees don't trust us, because our IT culture is fear-based and doesn't share power. Our employees don't trust them and consider them outsiders, even though they've been here now for seven years. We don't have access to their insights and perspectives.

When I recounted this part of my observation to Louisa, she responding in frustration:

> That's all true. But he's the one leading the integrations! Integrating employees to our culture? He's the one creating the fear! Working in silos? He retains control by keeping everyone separated! Talking to customers? His customers aren't returning his phone calls, because talking to him is unproductive. Everything he said is true, but he misses the

point completely that the constant in all this underperformance is *him*.

This raised questions in my mind about self-awareness, interest in others' opinions, and each of the characteristics we've been discussing.

By the time I had an opportunity to speak to David, however, Louisa had moved on to another company and was replaced by Jason. Jason was apprised of the fact that David was not on his predecessor's list for promotion and was targeted for performance improvement. I passed my observations along to Jason as well, and he even met with me to learn more.

And then Jason promoted David, to the shock and dismay of others.

This is a lament I've heard for twenty years from technology executives and entrepreneurs. Yes, there are always technical issues that need to be addressed, but technical issues can be addressed faster and with greater success if there is effective communication, collaboration, and trust between teams and functions. Too often, however, technology leaders make decisions about promotions based not on emotional or relational intelligence, but on technology expertise. Over the long term, this erodes the effectiveness of teams and prevents collaboration from going any further.

BUILDING A COLLABORATIVE CULTURE

A Chief Information Security Officer named Maria hired us to create a more collaborative culture during the recent pandemic. She was witnessing alienation, division, and separation between her clients and team, and she wanted to accelerate the resolution of her customers' most pressing issues. And she wanted to accomplish this while also building a healthier atmosphere of competition on her team. Together, we came up with a six-part plan that could accomplish both of her goals. The key elements of this plan were: recognizing the problem, aligning goals and actions, communicating clearly, making non-negotiable commitments, and assessing results honestly. Let's look at each of these elements to see how, together, they helped Maria achieve her goals.

Recognizing the Problem

The essential first step is for all interested parties to recognize why the current state of affairs is no longer acceptable. When people realize that the past isn't acceptable, it is easier to clarify the desired future state, usually over the course of the next eighteen to thirty-six months. When the problem is clearly articulated, the desired future state can be built on a common idea, hope, dream, or aspiration that animates all parties. If it's not, it's not the right future.

Collaboration takes time and can't be rushed. It's not like ordering a drive-through burger at a fast-food restaurant. It's more like partaking of a five-course meal at the best restaurant in town. Understanding the different functional areas and priorities of a team, as well as the world in which they live, allows all parties to relate to their stresses, understand the dynamics of their workloads, and appreciate customer demands. With this in place, you can craft a future state that wins the hearts and minds of all involved.

Aligning Goals and Actions

Alignment of goals and actions is also essential to collaboration. This alignment is best expressed using an automobile analogy. Think of the four wheels of your car as four aspects of traveling from point A to point B. The two front wheels represent strategy and execution. Without excellent execution, your strategy will fail. The two rear wheels represent talent and leadership. If you don't have the right leadership developing the talent, you can't execute well and, by extension, achieve your strategy. All these wheels need to be aligned. When they're not, you burn through extra fuel, wear out tires sooner, and exert more energy to cover the same distance. Or, even worse, you suffer a blowout and never make it to your desired destination.

The same holds true for collaboration within your business. Collaboration is required between marketing and sales, between R&D and engineering, between management and leadership, and between customer service and accounting. All of these are separate and distinct functions whose teams create excellence when passionately involved in their own work and the work of other functional areas.

Communicating Clearly

Not all words mean the same thing to all people. A soft bed means one thing to me, but it may mean something different to you. Spicy means something different to a native of Thailand than it does to a native of Scotland. And "as soon as possible" means something different to a team of engineers who are focused on perfection than it does to a sales team working to close a $1 million contract.

My experience in organizations has shown me that communication is often unclear and ambiguous. More than 70 percent of leaders think their communications to employees are clear, while fewer than 25 percent of front-line employees think their leaders' communications are clear.

Different teams and departments within companies each communicate through a preferred jargon that works for them. Sales and marketing speak a different language from R&D and engineering. Listening to these disparate groups trying to communicate is like listening to a group of French speakers chattering away with people who speak German. Since neither group understands the other's language, miscommunication and misunderstandings often occur. Crystal-clear communication requires that we drop the techno-babble of our respective areas and speak the language of the people with whom we need to communicate, which is often not our own.

Making Non-Negotiable Commitments

Each team of individuals collaborating to accomplish an important goal needs to be governed by a set of agreements that are non-negotiable. These agreements include the values, expectations, metrics of success, and behaviors that will achieve the desired future state.

And the behaviors that each team member will embrace and exemplify are included in these agreements as well. For example, one of my CIO clients drafted a desired future state that consisted of three simple words: enable customer success. After recognizing the problem the team was trying to solve and ensuring proper alignment of goals and actions, she asked each team member to develop a list of five behaviors they would practice daily. One person agreed to ask a customer for suggestions about how to improve their service offerings. Another committed to learning about one problem customers were having and working to solve it.

This behavioral component is vitally important. It allows everyone to link their desired behaviors with every appointment, email, or phone call on their calendar. These behaviors allow each member to be highly purposeful and intentional about collaborating and achieving their desired future.

Assessing Results Honestly

Maria renamed weekly team reviews "Tell the Truth Tuesdays." On these days, the meeting included a weekly review of the commitments made the preceding week, putting them under a microscope and discussing them in front of all interested parties. Were the team members collaborating? Had they adhered to their commitments as well as possible? During these discussions, the value of preserving personal dignity was of paramount importance. No one was ridiculed, called out, or shamed. They were asked and trusted to get back on track. They then made a non-negotiable agreement in front of everyone.

Building trust and respect, and preserving personal dignity were all important components of these truth-telling Tuesdays. Personal accountability and taking responsibility for commitments were front and center in these meetings. The result was deadlines met, commitments fulfilled, and healthy and productive mutual support among team members.

This after-action assessment brought important questions to the surface. What were the preceding week's successes and setbacks? What was intended? What was accomplished? What did team members learn? What would they do differently next week? All these questions were answered honestly by both the individuals and the group, resulting in many lessons learned and productive insights for the team.

Of course, getting an outsider's perspective is always extremely valuable as well—although this may seem self-serving coming from a coach. But my clients all tell me that they suffer from not having anyone with whom to discuss their individual challenges, trials, doubts, fears, and frustrations. They tell me they want and need an outsider's perspective to keep them from becoming too inwardly focused. They need someone external to challenge their assumptions, question their perceptions of reality, and collaborate from an unbiased perspective.

QUESTIONS

Here are some simple ways to improve the quality of your teams' collaboration by helping members of those teams improve themselves.

- Think of your direct reports. For how many of them do you know their hopes, dreams, and aspirations—professionally and personally?
- What are the specific talents, skills, and strengths of each of your direct reports?
- What would it look like for them to play to those strengths five, seven, or even ten times more effectively than they are doing today?

- What have you done to help them play to their strengths? What did you learn?
- Do your direct reports want to pursue excellence in their talents and skills?
- If yes, what's the payoff for them to do so at your organization?

If you ask these questions of your leadership team and get a confused look or even an "I'm good" response, don't stop there. Stay the course. Which brings us to the topic of the next chapter—determination.

CHAPTER 14

Determination— Never Give Up

Everybody knows that effort matters. What was reve-latory to me was how much it mattered.

ANGELA DUCKWORTH, AUTHOR OF *Grit*

In June 2005, I was persuaded by a good friend to join him in training for a triathlon, a fundraiser for cancer research that would include around seventy-five competitors committed to the cause. As someone who has been physically active all my life, I agreed. At the first meeting for participants, I learned this was not a sprint triathlon as I had thought—a quarter-mile swim, followed by a twelve-mile bike ride, followed by a three-mile run. This was a Half Ironman triathlon—a swim of one and a quarter miles, followed by a fifty-six-mile bike ride, ending in a run of just over thirteen miles. But I hid my shock because I found the stories of cancer survivors compelling, and said "I'm in."

The day of the race was particularly hot, with temperatures reaching over 90°. To make matters worse, the run at the end of the triathalon was to take place on a black asphalt road. Nonetheless, after twelve months of training, I stood on the shore ready to begin. Based on my training, my coach anticipated my finish time would be around six hours and forty-five minutes.

The all-enveloping heat brought me perilously close to quitting. I was simply not prepared for the heat. At times, I had to stop running and walk to keep from collapsing. I crossed the finish line in a disappointing eight hours and eight minutes, physically and mentally exhausted. I didn't want to talk to anyone. I just wanted to get back to my hotel room, jump in the shower, take a nap, and separate myself from the intensity of the sun, the run, and the race. Three hours later at the team celebration dinner, I met my team-mates for pizza and beer, shared war stories, and gained a glimpse of what I had accomplished. But it was there that I learned the same lesson Angela Duckworth shared at the opening of this chapter—a lesson that has remained with me for seventeen years.

Later that evening, we learned that one runner, Kathy, was still a mile and a half away from the finish line. Thirteen and a half hours after the race started, one runner was still on the course, by herself, running in the dark! The finish line had been dismantled. The time clock had been unplugged and packed away. It was completely dark and there would be no cheering crowd to witness Kathy's accomplishment. She would come across the finish line in the dark, alone.

When Kathy was a mile away from the finish line, four team members at the celebration dinner went out and ran the last mile with her, encouraging her and saying how amazed they were by her grit. It took Kathy another half hour to run that last mile. She was exhausted. She had been on the course for over fourteen hours when she finished the race. But what brings tears to my eyes all these years later was the moment Kathy was greeted by sixty-five of her fellow teammates when she crossed the now non-existent finish line. We surrounded her, lavished praise on her, and treated her as the elite-level team member she had become. She was grateful and elated that we were there for her, but more important for me and the rest of the team, we were in awe of what she had accomplished. Amid the hugs and high-fives were tears of joy and exhaustion.

TRUE GRIT

Kathy's accomplishment is inspiring for so many reasons. I didn't know her before the race, but seventeen years later I still remember her vividly for what she taught me about true grit. I learned six lessons from her that day: the importance of having a purpose, the importance of having a plan, the power of partnership, the power of keeping your promises, the strength gained through community, and the rewards you enjoy when you embrace a challenge. These six lessons can provide a powerful inspiration for leaders who want to create a culture of grit and determination, and a commitment never to give up during times of adversity. Let's look at each one of these lessons to see what insights they can give us into what it takes to be a leader with true grit.

Have a Purpose
Kathy had a purpose that she kept top of mind during the twelve months of training and the fourteen hours of her

race. She had a friend suffering from leukemia who was incapacitated by her treatments. Kathy saw the triathlon as a way to support her friend; she believed that her participation would encourage and uplift her. She felt that her running would give her friend the gift of encouragement to persevere through her treatments, as well as raise funds for cancer research. Kathy not only encouraged her friend; she also raised $15,000.

Have a Plan

Kathy was a fifty-five-year-old woman who wasn't built for triathlons, and she knew that to endure the race she would need a plan. The event's coaches provided her with what she needed. They outlined each week's training time and distances over fifty weeks. They walked her through the plan, told her what the challenges would be, encouraged her, and answered any questions she had. They told her: "If you follow this plan you *will* complete the race." That's what Kathy wanted. A plan and a process in which she could have confidence. Without a plan, she would have been rudderless and would never have crossed the finish line.

Have a Partner

Kathy connected with another member of the team to whom she could relate. They became training partners and were in lockstep for the duration of the training. They were mutually committed to each other's success, and partners in the truest sense. Their partnership was not a loose association. It was a formal promise to help each other rise up and live abundantly.

Keep Your Promises

Promises are non-negotiable agreements between two people. They are like vows, in the sense that there's a solemnity to them, and they are not to be taken lightly. The promises made between Kathy and her partner were process-oriented, not outcome-oriented. They each broke down the process of training, looked at their schedules, and promised to be with one another at certain dates and times. These promises sustained them, encouraged them, and helped them endure twelve months of rigorous training.

Join a Community

In addition to having a one-on-one partner, Kathy had the support of a community of seventy-five other teammates. The camaraderie of fellow community members struggling through the same heavy days of training provided strength for what was to come and a big dose of hope and optimism. She was a member of something much bigger than herself—a community of fellow athletes who gave her a sense of belonging—which, over time, created a sense of believing that she could do something that she had never done before. Everywhere she turned in the community, she found encouragement and a voice of hope that elevated her spirits.

Embrace the Challenge

Kathy knew the race would be difficult, but she welcomed it. She knew that, on the other side of the challenge, she would enjoy a reward aligned with her purpose. She knew that, at the end of the race, she would sit and tell her friend about it, and she knew what that would mean to her. Kathy was, in one sense, my first introduction to the concept of flow—that experience in which we have complete concentration, autonomy, clear goals, and a balance between risk and challenge.

Kathy knew that her skill level was not where it needed to be for a triathlon, but she had confidence in herself to remain focused on the one small thing that was in front of her at any given time. She forgot the outcome and stayed laser-focused on the next step in the process. And she knew that she was overcoming the challenge week by week.

QUESTIONS

Kathy's story can be an inspiration to us all. As you consider what she achieved, ask yourself these questions:

- Think back to the last time your team had to "gut out" a significant goal. What did you learn about your leadership and your team's grit and determination?
- What strategies do you employ to celebrate and encourage the accomplishment of goals never achieved before?
- After time off, how do you help employees recover from significant effort on a project?
- Do employees on your team exhibit a mindset of playing to win or playing not to lose? If they choose playing not to lose, how have you and your leadership team addressed this mindset?

The eight characteristics presented in these chapters hold the potential to be truly transformative and to give you the tools you need to live boldly, which is the topic of Part III.

PART III

Live Boldly

Introduction to Part III

Too many people today live lukewarm and timid lives. The gravitational pull toward average, toward feeling safe, toward fitting in, is powerful and difficult to resist. Although many have an intellectual understanding of what it means to commit to living a bold life as opposed to its opposite, many fewer have the fire in the belly to do that. This happens for three reasons.

- Others often criticize and detract from a commitment to live boldly. People with bold aspirations make those who lack boldness uncomfortable. To feel good about themselves, detractors work to make others feel small. But as Nelson Mandela said: "There's no passion to be found playing small and settling for a life that is less than the one you were capable of living."

- We live in a timid world where it is acceptable, and even at times preferred, to follow the herd and accept milquetoast relationships, mediocre results, and even lives of quiet desperation. That is the new normal and the world inhabited by many after our worldwide pandemic.

- We think that living boldly is something successful people do after becoming successful, as opposed to ways of living that lead to living successful lives.

Boldness does not require a radical departure from who you are or what you do. It doesn't require grand intentions of what you will do in the future or how you will change the course of human events. Boldness instead requires something subtle and approachable by normal human beings. Living boldly requires embracing the eight countercultural and radical characteristics you learned about in Part II and integrating them with the insights you gained in Part I.

It is important to understand, however, that without an idea, dream, hope, or aspiration that requires the help of others to accomplish, the strategies presented in Part III, although intellectually accurate and stimulating, will not be constructive in helping you to live or lead differently. These five powerful and actionable strategies will position you as a true difference-maker known for promoting real and positive change.

CHAPTER 15

The Boldness Paradox

If we don't change, we don't grow. If we don't grow,
we aren't really living.

GAIL SHEEHY

Change is certain, but growth is optional. That's the paradox of living boldly. Cultivating the courage to overcome fear and lean into its transformational power is essential for growth, but that requires bold action. It requires that we accept change as a precondition for growth, and acknowledge that what worked for us in the past won't move us forward on the path to greatness. It is only by adopting a strategy of "failing forward faster," however, that we can manage change in a way that allows us to grow in our personal and professional lives.

Change is happening at an unprecedented rate. In what became known as Moore's Law, Gordon Moore warned in 1965 that the number of transistors on microchips would double roughly every two years—a prospect that promised that computers would become significantly faster, smaller, and more efficient at a rate that increased exponentially over time.[24] And we have seen the impact of this rate of increase in very real ways over the last fifty years.

Now some scientists are warning that the power of artificial intelligence (AI) will grow *750-fold* over the next twenty-four months! Eleven months ago, an AI app passed the bar exam in the lowest 10 percent of the class. Eleven months later, that ranking had risen to the *top* 10 percent. Some are concerned about this exponential increase, warning that we don't have the wisdom or skills to manage this rate of change and growth.

Jack Welch pointed out the dangers implicit in this rapidly accelerating rate of change: "If the rate of change on the outside exceeds the rate of change on the inside, the end is near."[25] But these warnings beg the question of whether we will even be able to comprehend and accept that rate of change. And that's the central theme of this chapter. If change is certain, but growth is optional, do we have the capability to choose how we'll respond to change of this magnitude?

CHANGE OR DIE

One of the more interesting analyses of change that I have read over the last twenty years appeared in a pivotal 2005 *Fast Company* article by Alan Deutschman entitled "Change or Die." Deutschman wrote convincingly about resistance to change, beginning with this challenging question: "If you were presented with the choice of changing your behavior or dying, which one would you choose?"[26] If you're like me, you probably answered: "That's a dumb question. Of course, I'd choose to change my behavior over dying." But you'd be wrong. The odds of us changing our behavior when given this choice are nine to one. That's nine to one *against us!*

At a global innovation conference in the early 2000s, thinkers worldwide met to propose solutions to "big problems." First they tackled healthcare. At the time of the conference, the United States spent $1.8 trillion a year on healthcare—15 percent of our GDP. Today, we spend $4.3 trillion—18.3 percent of our GDP. That means we spend $12,419 per person annually on healthcare. Yet our healthcare is rated thirtieth in quality worldwide.[27] Many thought then, as they do now, that the solution to this problem was some technical innovation or perhaps genetic sequencing, both of which would have a significant impact on the quality and delivery of healthcare. But that wasn't the solution then—or today.

The most compelling case made at the conference was that a disproportionate amount of our healthcare dollars are allocated to a small percentage of people, and most of the conditions being treated are rooted in behavioral choices. Ironically, it is how we live our lives that is going to kill us.

One presenter pointed out that many studies have demonstrated that five behavioral issues consume 80 percent of the healthcare budget.[28] We all know what they are and maybe even engage in some of them ourselves. We smoke too much; we drink too much; we have too much stress in our lives; we exercise too little; and we eat unhealthy diets. We make really bad healthcare decisions.

The knockout blow in the argument was delivered by the CEO at Johns Hopkins University Medical Center. He observed that there were 600,000 patients with heart disease so severe that they needed surgery—either bypass surgery or angioplasty. The average cost of these surgeries at the time was $30,000, resulting in a total cost of $18 billion. Yet today, these surgeries cost on average $75,345, and they still don't eliminate heart disease. They just reduce the immediate pain and lower the risk, so that the necessary behavioral changes can occur.[29]

This CEO claimed that many patients could avoid the return of pain and the need to repeat the surgery—not to mention correct the course of their heart disease before it kills them—by adopting healthier lifestyles. But very few do. Multiple studies show that, two years post-surgery, 90 percent of those who had coronary-artery bypass surgery have not changed their lifestyles. I repeat. Nine out of ten people who have had heart surgery refuse to change their lifestyles to address their heart conditions.

I find that hard to believe. How is it possible that respected healthcare providers can tell patients that, if they don't change their behavior, they will die, and yet two years later, those patients indulge in the same behaviors that warranted the warning in the first place? I wanted to believe there was a missing gene in those who refused to make these changes and that I was smarter than that. I wanted to think that I had more discipline, a better and more athletic fitness level, and more willpower than they did. But that wasn't the case. When I was in the grip of my own fear-based health crisis, I maintained the status quo for two years.

After turning forty-five, I gained fifteen pounds—all of which seemed to have found a home around my waist. This was a disproportionate amount of weight for me to carry on my frame in one place. My physician told me that my cholesterol was way too high. With a family history of heart disease, he warned, this issue really needed to be addressed. Several rounds of blood work confirmed my dangerously high cholesterol levels and prompted a repeat of my doctor's warnings. Two years later, I was in the same spot I had been two years earlier. I knew what to do. I had spent ten years in the healthcare field and had been an athletic trainer, a runner, and a triathlete at times. I knew what to do. I just was not taking action.

Keep in mind that it's not as if the issue at hand was hidden from me. I saw my waistline daily, reminding me of my doctor's warnings. Reluctantly and halfheartedly, I complained about my symptoms to my wife, but I still ate potato chips (salt and fat are heavenly, just in case you don't know) and my favorite candy. Halloween at our house was never for the kids. It was always for me. I hid the number of times I ate candy from my wife. And it wasn't even good candy—just cheap pedestrian candy.

I was out of control and relying heavily on my skills as an excellent complainer. But nothing changed. I jokingly told myself that an intervention was necessary and even looked up the twelve steps of Alcoholics Anonymous to see if there was something I needed to learn. I have to admit that, in many ways, I *was* the person written about in Deutschman's article. I found myself looking in the mirror and knowing that my resistance to change was damaging my health and wellness. And then I remembered something mentioned in the article.

CHANGE AND LIVE

The individuals in the study who reversed their heart disease and were most successful in changing their behavior followed a protocol developed by Dean Ornish, founder of the Preventative Medicine Research Institute in Sausalito, California.[30] His solution, which was somewhat radical, relied on three elements: emphasizing feelings over facts, total immersion tactics, and solid support.

Ornish stopped talking to his patients just about the facts of their conditions and started talking to them about their feelings. He asked prospective patients how they currently felt and how they envisioned that living fully and abundantly would feel. When people began to envision the possibility of a pain-free walk up the stairs or participation in activities they couldn't presently enjoy, they became open to learning more. Their fear was reduced and their willingness to listen increased.

Ornish dramatically shifted his patients to a primarily vegetarian diet, with only 10 percent of their calories coming from fat. And he didn't slowly ramp up the introduction of this diet. He followed a strategy of total immersion. His patients went from one way of eating to another overnight. He did this because he knew that, in as little as three weeks, they would lose enough weight to start to see results and that this would make their continued adherence to the diet more likely, and maybe even more palatable.

Finally, Ornish enrolled patients in a twice-weekly support group led by a psychologist who taught them how to meditate, relax, do yoga, and exercise aerobically. His program lasted a year, but after three years, 77 percent of patients were still enrolled in it. That's a great success rate. On the other hand, 90 percent of those with heart disease who were left to their own devices failed to implement change. They still had the sword of Damocles hanging over their heads.

When I finally admitted that I couldn't address my own health issues alone, I hired a nutritionist and, in a point-of-no-return moment, paid for her services in advance. I now had a detailed nutrition plan and a sixteen-week exercise program. I submitted myself to accountability calls and weigh-ins. And perhaps most uncomfortable of all, I had pictures taken of me in my boxers. Sixteen weeks later, I had dropped eight pounds and reduced my body fat by 2.5 percent. That may not seem like a massive amount of weight, but it was a lot on my frame. The best part is that I started to enjoy food again and stopped bingeing on junk food. I felt in control and empowered by the process.

So, what does all this mean for us here?

THE GROWTH CURVE

One of my early mentors in the leadership and coaching world was a psychiatrist turned organizational-development consultant named Peter Robertson, founder and CEO of Human Insight and author of the book *Always Change a Winning Team*.[31]

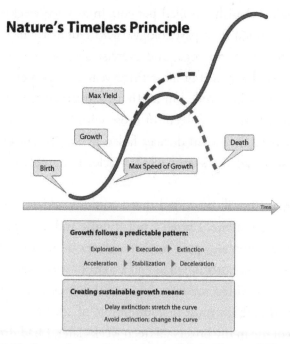

Figure 1. The "growth curve," sometimes called the "S curve," illustrating the natural capacity we all have to implement change by jumping from one growth curve to another.

When I first met Peter, he shared his experience and thinking about a change model that is based in common sense, but not used in common practice. This model, called the "growth curve" and sometimes referred to as the "S curve," was discussed in the book *Blueprint to a Billion*.[32] It consists of a series of integrated s-shaped curves that demonstrate the natural capacity we all have to implement change by jumping from one growth curve to another (see Figure 1). In other words, growth follows a natural and predictable pattern.

According to this model, everything in nature goes through a period of birth, growth, decay, and eventually death. That holds true for plants, animals, textbooks, business plans, and, yes, human beings. A computer-science textbook written five years ago is obsolete today. Businesses start up, grow, succeed, and fail following patterns that develop in the underlying culture—including market pressures, economic fluctuations, societal changes, disease, and wars. Careers and life paths grow and change with the situations and environments in which they operate.

One of my clients is the provost of a prominent university. In the first ten months of her tenure, she went through a massive growth cycle because of the relationships she was developing and the unrelenting demands made on her to learn quickly about the culture and intricacies of her job. When I conducted interviews for our strategic leadership review, I found that she had made exponential progress in building strategic partnerships across the campus. The recognition and praise she received confirmed that the early "birthing" stage of the growth curve was paying dividends, and that she was accelerating her way up the curve. Seeing this made more change palatable and welcome. Her fear was reduced considerably.

In most cases, we can extend growth by either jumping to another growth curve or extending our existing curve. As my client recognized, both options require courage. For change to be successful, however, you must have the heart, desire, or love for the change, otherwise it will fail.

You and I will die. We were born, and will hopefully have gone through a seventy-, eighty-, or maybe even a ninety-year life cycle. At some point, we'll start to slow down and decay, and eventually we'll die. This is not meant to be morbid. Rather it is meant as a gentle reminder that, just like textbooks, businesses, leaders, and teams, we all go through changes in the natural order of things. And we can go through the same kinds of changes in our behaviors and in our lives if we have the will and a process to do so. We can jump to another growth curve and reinvent ourselves. But it's a courageous act to leave behind one level of success and jump to another curve. It requires that we acknowledge that we need to do things differently.

All growth starts by telling the truth of where we are today. Many of us know that truth. We just want to avoid it. Our past successes become so captivating that we can't seem to turn our backs on them. Our successes and failures influence and shape what we do in the future, but the future doesn't have to be a carbon copy of what has gone before. We need what Carol Dweck called a "growth mindset"—one that is not afraid of change because of an innate belief that we can figure out how to learn and grow in ways that serve us best.[33] In his book *What Got You Here Won't Get You There*, Marshall Goldsmith argued for this kind of change, pointing out that you can learn from the things that have made you successful in the past, but you can't rely on them to sustain you for the entirety of your career.[34]

DYING TO CHANGE

The truth is that, in order for you to live boldly, the old you has to die before a new you can be born. But rest assured that the death we're discussing here is not always as dramatic as a physical one. It can be the death of a leadership role, a service offering, or a business. Think of all the big-name enterprises that have fallen by the wayside in recent years. Think of Liz Truss, who has the honor of being the shortest-serving Prime Minster of the UK, serving for only forty-nine days. Think of the demise of creative careers—of artists and actors who learn that no one wants to buy their albums or cast them in TV series or films. Think of all the TV shows that are canceled for low ratings. And for those of us in leadership roles, death comes when people lose confidence in our leadership and no longer trust us or are unwilling to follow our lead.

The growth-curve model reminds us that we can jump to another curve with courage. Overcoming the fear associated with leaving one curve and jumping to another is a deeply courageous act, because it requires the deep transformational work of changing our perspective, our mindset, our identity, and, ultimately, our behavior. This change is successful when leaders, teams, or businesses see the writing on the wall and love their customers, employees, and work in such a deeply personal way that they're willing to turn away from what's made them successful in the past because it's no longer working.

You may think you would change if you were told your career was on life support and needed a life-saving surgery. And I hope you're right. Unfortunately, we all tend to think that, if we tweak some things around the edges and convince ourselves that we are doing the meaningful work necessary to be successful, we can carry on as we are. We're creatures of habit. We have a narrow operating band that works like a thermostat that is kept between sixty-nine and seventy-one degrees. We want to be comfortable. Moving out of our comfort zones and changing is scary for many of us. But transformational change is not something to which we can become accustomed.

Sometimes the changes we undertake are not of our own choosing. Sometimes they are thrust upon us. In these moments, change can be hard, and sometimes we need a truth-teller we trust and respect in our corner to help us through. Do you have a truth-teller? If not, chances are you need one in order to make the jump in your leadership required to inspire greatness in others.

QUESTIONS

See how well you are managing your own growth curve by answering these questions. Then think about what your answers mean for the likelihood that you are prepared to implement transformational change.

- What one area of your leadership will kill your credibility and effectiveness if you don't change?
- What area of your leadership would an outside expert you trust and respect not characterize as embodying greatness?
- In what area of your organization do your customers expect or deserve greatness, but aren't receiving it?
- What leadership behaviors have you and your team promised to exhibit to foster a market-differentiating or dominance culture?

In order to live boldly, you have to move from one way of living to another. Once you accept that what got you here will not get you where you want to go, I think you will find the next chapter liberating. Because if you are not living purposefully, you are living accidentally. And an accidental life will never lead to greatness.

CHAPTER 16

A Purposeful Life

Your vision will become clear only when you can look into your own heart. Who looks outside, dreams; who looks inside, awakens.

CARL JUNG

The second step in living boldly is the jumping-off point for individual and organizational greatness. This chapter will help you peel back the layers of your thinking and shed light on the hopes, dreams, and aspirations you have for your work and personal life—hopes, dreams, and aspirations that you don't want to let go unfulfilled.

Think about it. I'd wager that the most successful people you know, both personally and professionally, live their lives on purpose, as opposed to accidentally. An accidental professional life is a waste of talent and skill, and leads to mediocrity and stagnation. An accidental personal life limits your level of engagement with and enjoyment of life, and leads to disengagement and lower levels of fulfillment.

Having a leadership purpose sets a course for you as a leader. It provides direction and acts as your guardrails so you can see what you should and shouldn't do. This aligns closely with what you learned in chapter 12 about integrity, because a purposeful life exemplifies your credibility and authenticity. But to live a purposeful life, you first have to understand the main elements of purpose and just how they can help you achieve excellence, both professionally and personally.

LIVING PURPOSEFULLY

Purpose is found at the intersection of love, talent, and value. These are the three dimensions of greatness in leadership. In order to clarify your purpose, you have to gain a deep understanding of how your unique passions, talents, and skills create value for you, for your customers, for your organization, and for your family and community. Let's take a closer look at these three paths to see how successfully you are moving forward on your journey to living purposefully.

Love

At the heart of greatness lies love for customers, for projects, or for ideals. We can love our work, or we can love the work we do. These two things may seem the same, but they are not. While different, however, they're not mutually exclusive. Through your love of your work, you are motivated to overcome challenges and achieve what you desire the most. When you're driven to accomplish what you see as a noble and uplifting future, work ceases to be a four-letter word.

As we saw in Part I, love is a key component of engagement and fulfillment. Here are some questions that no one but you can answer. Together, your answers form a significant part of your leadership purpose. Don't answer them mechanically and transactionally. Instead, take the time to think through your responses and confirm that they accurately describe you at work.

- What part of my job do I love doing? Why?
- What part of my work do I find most rewarding?
- What is the one idea, hope, dream, or aspiration regarding my work that has grabbed hold of me and won't let go?
- Would I find my work less fulfilling if there were one aspect of it that I was no longer able to do? What aspect is that?

Talent

Where do your strengths lie? To answer this question, begin by identifying what you do well for your organization. In what ways do you effectively serve your customers and employees? Thinking about your talent also provides you with an opportunity to identify areas for further development.

If you need help answering the questions below, refer back to any strengths-based assessments you may have done. Or check out tools like the CliftonStrengths Finder or the High5 assessment.[35] If you use these assessments, be sure to link the strengths you list directly back to a part of your work.

- What are the five most important talents and skills I bring to my team and organization?
- What is my proudest contribution and/or accomplishment? Why?

- For what part of my work do I receive the most compliments?
- What are five work activities in which I take great pride?
- In what part of my job do I want to pursue excellence?

Value
The value you create is not the input side of the purpose equation; it's the output side. It's the value a customer or your organization receives from you being on the team. To determine the value you provide, ask yourself these questions:

- In my professional life, what are the most valuable contributions I make to my customers, my colleagues or coworkers, and my organization?
- What aspects of my work are distinctive? What differentiates me from my colleagues who have the same role?
- If I were no longer able to do some aspect of my work, would my customers be bitterly disappointed? What aspect would that be?
- How can I increase the value I bring to my organization?

Mapping the Intersection
To determine where love, talent, and value intersect for you—to clarify your purpose—complete these three statements:

- My three most significant insights are _____.
- When I review my three dimensions of purpose, I see that I excel both technically and relationally at _____.
- The most important thing I want to accomplish is _____.

Consider the insights you've gleaned. What idea is particularly meaningful to you? Your insights will point you in a tentative direction of your leadership purpose.

To articulate your purpose, write an initial purpose statement that reflects your love contribution, your talent contribution, and your value contribution. You can use the template below or you can write your purpose statement in your own words.

> *I help (your ideal customer) (do something) so they can achieve (what) _____.*

For example:

> *We help executives, entrepreneurs, and investors transform human potential into inspired performance so they can accelerate business value.*

Once you have drafted your purpose statement, consider how it fits your situation. What, if any, changes will make it a better fit for your leadership?

It can help to discuss your purpose with someone you trust and respect. Does it resonate in the same way with you and with them? Keep in mind that your purpose statement is not being carved into marble tablets. It's being written in pencil and will change over time until you arrive at one that you know reflects who you are.

Once you've clarified your purpose, an important next step is to evaluate how well you are living it. As we have seen, the impact your activities have on others informs perceptions about your leadership. For what are you known? Would a co-worker be able to infer your purpose from working with you? The answers to these questions will help point you toward your personal brand.

YOUR PERSONAL BRAND

Brands are among the most strategic assets of an organization. They have tangible, financial value both for your organization and for your personal career goals. And you have a personal brand as well, one that *personifies* your leadership purpose. But when what you personify is not aligned with your purpose, your credibility is jeopardized, your effectiveness is compromised, and others' perceptions of you may not be what you would like them to be.

In other words, it's not enough just to clarify your purpose, you have to personify it. When your actions don't embody your purpose, you're living incongruently. And congruence between what you want to create for your leadership—your purpose—and what you personify—your personal brand—is a vital component of transformational leadership.

Personifying your purpose is a conscientious act. When you consider whether your behaviors and purpose are aligned, you begin to clarify your personal brand. But this can be a complex process that requires a lot of self-reflection.

In the next activity, we'll explore the three elements that help to make up your personal brand—what I call your default brand, your desired brand, and your designed brand—to see how they can exemplify your purpose and help you to flourish professionally. We'll break this down into six steps.

Step 1

First, let's define your default brand. This is your starting point for building your leadership brand. Write down four words or phrases that you believe best describe your leadership today. Don't overthink this. Simply capture what you see as the essence of your leadership. For what do you believe you are known?

Step 2

Now consider these leadership qualities in terms of your behaviors. What do you do at work that supports your leadership goals? What behaviors do you exhibit that don't? For example, perhaps you see yourself as an open communicator, yet you recognize that you sometimes interrupt or multitask during conversations. A candid self-assessment can provide insights into your default brand. Write down four words or phrases that summarize your leadership behaviors.

Step 3

Now write a description of what you perceive to be your leadership qualities. Distill this down to the fewest words possible. To do so, look at the lists you created in the first two steps. Then whittle those down to the four or five words that best represent your current leadership. This is your default brand.

Step 4

Determine if there's a gap between the leadership descriptors you identified as your purpose, and the behaviors you exhibit. Ask yourself the following questions:

- Am I being seen in ways consistent with my goals and aspirations?
- What are the upside and downside to my leadership brand/reputation?
- Am I excited about the words used to describe me, or am I neutral?

Step 5

Now, let's define your desired brand. Your desired brand is what you *want* to be known for. It is, as the term suggests, the way you want people to see you, know you, and think of you. Your desired brand is less about logic. It articulates the highest hopes and aspirations you have for yourself and your leadership. Start by answering the following questions:

- What is it that I want to be known for?
- What traits, characteristics, and/or values are essential or non-negotiable to me?

Step 6

Now you can define your designed brand. This is the brand you want to put into action. Think about what you identified as your desired brand, then ask yourself how you can exemplify that brand in your actions and behaviors. What behaviors will you exhibit in order to be seen as your desired brand? Are these behaviors distinctive, or simply necessary for fulfilling your role? Write your designed brand below.

As we saw in chapter 8, we all have blind spots when it comes to assessing our own behaviors and how we're perceived by others. For more information on activities to help you better understand how you're perceived, you can go to my website at *clarisconsulting.net.*

QUESTIONS

Take a few minutes to consider the insights you have gained from this chapter and what their immediate impacts are on your living boldly.. Then write down your answers to these questions:

- What one thing will I implement as a result of this chapter?
- In what areas am I feeling successful?
- With what am I experiencing difficulty?
- How am I adding value to my organization/team?
- What is the most significant impact this chapter has had on me?

Living your purpose and your brand are both rooted in your identity as a leader. In the next chapter, you'll learn how to reframe your past identity, claim your future identity, and begin living that future identity today.

CHAPTER 17

Your Future Self

You have to be willing to go to war with yourself and create a whole new identity.

DAVID GOGGINS

Your identity—who you believe you are—influences your actions, your decisions, your impact on others, and your professional and personal definitions of success. When your identity prevents you from thinking highly of yourself, your perception of what's possible is limited. In this chapter, we'll explore what it takes to move forward on the path to identity transformation, and how that can lead you to greatness.

Your identity encompasses all the memories, experiences, and relationships you've ever had. It constitutes the deep-felt experience of who you are at your core. Changing your identity requires that you tell yourself the truth about your beliefs, your perceptions, and your views of yourself and the world around you.

Imagine growing up in poverty with a drug-addicted mother and an alcoholic father who beat you for looking the wrong way. This was the experience of a homeless man I met in Seattle. His identity was one of worthlessness. And this aligned with his lived experience. He used drugs and alcohol to medicate himself and separate himself from the painful experience of being raised by addicted parents.

But the fact is that our lived experiences today and our past experiences are not an accurate representation of who we are. They shape our lives in profound ways. But they do not irrevocably determine the essence of who we are. As David Goggins notes in the quote that opens this chapter, you have to be willing to go to war with yourself and create a new identity. War may seem like a strong word here, but there are times when we go through internal battles between what we believe to be true and what the world says is true.

The past experiences of the homeless man in Seattle, as well as my own and yours, have planted seeds in the fertile soil of our imaginations—ideas and beliefs about who we are and what we are worthy of in this world. Those roots go deep and are as challenging to remove as bamboo from a garden. But, as we saw in the last chapter, you can change those ideas and beliefs. And above all, you can change your behaviors. You can *shapeshift* into a new identity that better serves your life's purpose.

SHAPESHIFTING

I can tell you from personal experience that shifting an identity that is woven into every nook and cranny of who you are is, in fact, like a war. In my case, it was a battle between my good-and-better angel on one side and the darkest characters in *Lord of the Rings* on the other. That's not hyperbole, but more a testament to the wisdom of J. R. R. Tolkien's descripton of the battle between good and evil and the hero's journey. But just because something is hard, that doesn't mean that we shouldn't try to achieve it.

My identity has shaped my whole life trajectory. It is rooted in being an immigrant, in witnessing race relations in the deep South in the 1960s, and in being a white, middle-aged male. I am a homeowner, a husband, a dog-lover, a high-performance coach, and a Catholic. I am fit and healthy and I love barbecue. And I am a bourbon-loving Bohemian. Okay, Bohemian may be little strong—but I defintely love bourbon and barbecue.

I am in love with my wife. I love learning and pursuing growth in all areas of life. I love connecting with people and having deep conversations about issues that matter. I love storytelling, adventure, and travel, and am passionate about seeking out new experiences of all sorts. I enjoy a level of professional success that affords my family a substantial level of comfort.

These traits are only part of my identity, however. They constitute the identity I want to share publicly, because they make me look well-rounded, self-aware, smart, and successful. But a shadow identity lies deep in my experience that has had an outsized influence on my personal and professional life. I worked hard to keep it in check for over thirty years, but this became so exhausting that I finally said: "Enough is enough."

My shadow identity is someone who "felt but didn't express" an entitlement to privileged treatment. I believed that

I deserved to win at the expense of others. I found the life story of Scottish industrialist Andrew Carnegie, who wrestled wealth away from others to enrich himself, worthy of praise and study. I have had problems with attention and focus since the age of twelve, leading to my being called disruptive, distracting, disrespectful, compulsive, unfocused, dumb, and lazy. This, in turn, caused me to grow up with low trust in myself and in others. I also identify with being insecure and seeking attention that sometimes borders on a need for adoration from friends, family, and even clients and colleagues. This shadow side of my identity shows up when I feel out of my comfort zone, tired, or threatened.

Why is it important to share this backstory in a book about pursuing greatness and living boldly? Because it is only when you see both the upside and the downside of your identity that you can craft and communicate a holistic identity that projects the best and brightest expression of who you are at your core. This is the identity you want to create as a leader. We'll talk about how to do that in the next chapter. For now, I just want to help you understand your assumptions about yourself, how you explain yourself to yourself, and how you live that explanation in the world of work.

A word of caution. Your shadow identity does not want to give up control or go quietly into the good night! For that to happen, you need a process to help subdue your shadow and elevate your ideal future identity instead. For I am of the firm conviction that, when you elevate your identity, you elevate the impact you have on others, which in turn moves you forward on the path to greatness.

In my case, I adopted a methodology called Rational Emotive Behavior Therapy (REBT) that helped me develop alternative explanations and emotions associated with events.[36] This helped me discharge negative emotions and created a new narrative that held me less hostage to the triggering event. This experience led me to formulate a three-part process that can help you challenge your own assumptions and gain mastery of your mindset so that you can shapeshift into an identity that better serves your life purpose. It consists of reframing your past, reclaiming your future, and recalibrating your present.

REFRAMING YOUR PAST

I once heard that having a positive mental attitude does not guarantee a positive outcome, but having a negative attitude certainly guarantees a negative one. So it follows that, while thinking positively may not guarantee our success, it certainly greases the skids for us to be successful.

Focusing on what's positive helps you become more resilient, positively shaping your short-term behavior and your character over the long term. But adversity and things not going as planned are a normal part of life, and, in my experience, more of a catalyst for growth than success. Adversity can be our greatest teacher and can teach those we lead how to lead. That's why renowned basketball coach John Wooden claimed: "Sports don't build character; they reveal it."[37] By extension, adversity may not build character, but it can certainly reveal it.

While training for my Half Ironman triathlon, I experienced a panic attack during my first open-water swim. It was so powerful that I drove home afterward crying from exhaustion and convinced that, after eleven months of training, I would give up and not participate in the race. My wife, a consummate athlete in her own right, suggested speaking with a sports psychologist before making that decision. Paraphrasing the Greek Stoic philosopher Epictetus, he told me that all of the experiences I'd had with my training were not happening *to* me; they were happening *for* me. My training results were not the byproduct of a mysterious outside force trying to stifle my success and satisfaction. They were pointing to a problem in my training. If I fixed the problem, I'd avoid the panic attacks. In other words, we have the option to learn from all our experiences and use them to help us get better.

The wisdom I gained from this experience had an important impact on my general thinking about life. I learned that all of our experiences—no matter how tragic or traumatic—can teach us. It is only when we reject these lessons that we become victims.

When I internalized this, my view of learning and growth changed. I adopted more of what Carol Dweck called a "growth mindset." I learned that my experiences were catalysts for growth and learning, and that I could convert negative and uncomfortable experiences into healthy and positive ones with the right tools. In psychology, this is called "post-traumatic growth" (PTG).

PTG is a theory developed in the 1990s by psychologists Richard Tedeschi and Lawrence Calhoun that explains the transformation that is possible when we see negative, painful, and traumatic experiences through a new and more positive lens. The theory suggests that people who endure psychological struggle after a physical or mental event can often see positive growth afterward. "People develop new understandings of themselves, the world they live in, how to relate to other people, the kind of future they might have, and a better understanding of how to live life," Tedeschi claims.[38] This is important for us as leaders and coaches, because our response to adversity shapes what others do when the yogurt hits the fan.

Seeing past adverse events in a different light and learning from that change in perspective can be a game-changer for us individually, for our teams, and for our organizations. I had the choice to convert the negative traumatic experience of having men show up at my parents' door to repossess our furniture into one of being deeply committed to making "Yes, I can" choices. And now I am grateful for the wisdom and insight I gained to make choices aligned with my values, my commitment to my family, and my dream of being financially secure.

As a leader, do your responses to adversity inspire greatness in you and others? If your answer is less than enthusiastic and you want to change your response, try identifying the triggering event and converting it into a learning experience that transforms it into the best and most positive experience possible.

RECLAIMING YOUR FUTURE

To have high hopes for the future, you must have a hope, a dream, an aspiration, or a big idea that has grabbed hold of you and prompted you to reply with a bold and unequivocal "yes." Big dreams and aspirations of the sort you identified in Part I trigger responses like: "Under no circumstances will I take no for an answer." There's no escape when a big hope, or dream, or aspiration grabs hold of you. When you say you will accomplish it, you reclaim the idealized future you want most.

Current research on the future self by Hal Hershfield and Benjamin Hardy bear this out. Our future self, they tell us, is vastly different from our past self. Our future self is not simply an extrapolation of who we will be based on who we are today or who we have been in the past. Our future self is detached from our present and past selves and claims a future that brings us alive.[39]

In five years, your future self will look very different from who you are today, but that shouldn't scare you or discourage you from pursuing it. Reclaiming your future self helps you recognize that you can choose and claim a future dramatically different from who you are today. This starts with articulating the experience you envision in a multisensory way. What does your future look like? What does it feel like and sound like? What does it smell like and taste like? Envisioning your future like this plays tricks on your brain. The moment you see your future with all of your senses, your brain believes it's real—no longer a visualization, but reality. And as Stephen Covey told us, this reality is created first in your mind's eye before it's created in the real world. That's not new age mumbo jumbo. That's the psychology of high performance.

RECALIBRATING YOUR PRESENT

Recalibrating your present requires that you recognize what you should *stop* doing and acknowledge what you should *start* doing. This involves seeing how your future self thinks and behaves, and aligning your current behavior with the behavior of your future self.

What does your future self hope for you? What creates a deep sense of satisfaction and success for your future self? Identify the areas of your future self that need to be brought into the present and take one small step to create that state. Make it behavioral, actionable, and repeatable. Don't try to accomplish everything at once. Instead, identify a mindset you can change or a belief you can transform or a behavior you can shift that will attract your future self. Then double down on it.

David Goggins's metaphor of battle and war can be off-putting. But I have retained that language here because, as you've read in the examples of the people with whom I've worked, there's a battle raging between their better and evil angels. They are engaged in a conflict between their tentative, timid, uncertain—and yes, even fearful—selves and the army of their bold and limit-busting selves. There's a war unfolding; make no mistake about it. The question is, can you tell yourself the truth about it?

QUESTIONS

Are you willing to do battle to live boldly? If you are, here are six bold identity-changing questions you can ask yourself.

- When you think of the life you want to live five, ten, or twenty years in the future, how do you describe it? Can you describe it with crystal clarity?
- What one part of your past is most in need of an identity change? From what to what?

- Is the future you that you want significantly "bigger" than the current you? If not, why not?
- Are you willing to do battle to achieve the future you?
- What is the one audacious act you've put off doing that you are no longer willing to leave undone?
- If living boldly means finding something for which you're willing to die, what is that for you?

In the next chapter, I'll share with you how one man raised his expectations for his work and became the winningest member of his profession.

CHAPTER 18

Pursuing the Impossible

It always seems impossible until it's done.

NELSON MANDELA

Our thinking is too often restricted by our past experiences and what we think we're capable of achieving. But we can, with the right mindset and the right skills, learn how to think bigger and become a catalyst for greatness.

Ben Feldman was an insurance agent—but not just any insurance agent. He was, without hesitation, one of the most successful insurance agents in the last seventy-five years. When he began his career in 1942 at the age of thirty, he wanted to be the very best at helping families, individuals, and business owners solve difficult financial problems. What's astounding is that Ben personally sold *$1.8 billion* worth of life insurance! He was the first agent ever to sell $100 million of life insurance in a single year. Thirty years into his career, he was selling more insurance himself than 83 percent of the 1,800 insurance companies serving America at that time.[40] If you had told 99.9 percent of all insurance agents at the time that they could achieve the same level of success, the response would probably have been a resounding: "That's impossible."

But thinking small was simply not in Ben's DNA. He was a bold game-changer who set seemingly unattainable goals and then met them by breaking each one down into the smaller, actionable behaviors necessary to be successful. Ben was a passionate and innovative man with an unbelievable work ethic who worked seven days a week, twelve hours a day. Was he driven? Yes. But he was also drawn—drawn to making a difference in his clients' lives. He loved them and, whenever he saw an opportunity to make a difference, he made the effort. The key to his success is that he was both a people and a process person. He always had a process for achieving what he defined as excellence. When asked about his success, he said: "If you ever have a problem, turn it into a process, and you won't have a problem anymore."

Do you have a process for pursuing greatness? In addition to working hard, do you know who you need to be or become in order to achieve the goals you've said are important to you? Have you defined the what, where, when, how, and why of your process? LeBron James and Tom Brady both had processes for achieving greatness in their respective fields. Their success was never accidental; they didn't win the "greatness lottery." They were crystal clear about what they wanted to achieve at a specific time in the future, what they would have to do to achieve it, and who they needed to be to succeed.

There's always a process you can implement in order to achieve your boldest goals. Someone, somewhere, has been successful doing exactly what you want to do. And you can replicate that process, personalize it, and customize it to meet your situation. You just have to avoid a couple of key pitfalls: reinventing the wheel and setting low standards.

DON'T REINVENT THE WHEEL

There are role models and exemplars in every industry. If you are a university president, you likely have a role model in your field to whom you look for inspiration. Whether you're an executive coach, a high school teacher, or the operator of a ten-unit car wash, there are always others at the pinnacle of success that you can look to as role models. If you're in the same industry or association, you can build a relationship with them and ask them what they do that makes them so successful. What are the principles by which they operate? What are the habits or processes they use?

But be careful of social-media experts. Most of them are charlatans who promise a quick fix. They tell us that, if we follow their three simple steps or eat certain magic foods, we'll be transformed from our normal everyday selves into superstars. My experience is that 99.9 percent of these claims are made by opportunists who are trying to profit by saying there's a quick fix or an easy path to success. I equate their efficacy to what I call "spraying and praying." They spray high-octane sound bites and pray that they work. Nine times out of ten they don't. These kinds of "do this" schemes neglect the "become this" aspects of personal change and growth. True personal transformation is a state of being that can't be achieved by subscribing to some off-the-shelf bromide.

Let's be clear. There are no quick paths to greatness; you can't "hack" into greatness. Simply put, there's nothing sexy about pursuing greatness. My experience has taught me that pursuing or coaching greatness is rooted in a passion for others, or a game, or a job, or an audience, or solving problems. By extension, this makes love the jumping-off point for greatness. Any process that's rooted in uninspiring goals or that lacks a passion aligned with your deepest desires is a process that will create boredom and yield marginal results.

When I needed new business processes, I turned to two brilliant coaches who had implemented replicable and actionable processes that solved a pressing problem I had. I didn't reinvent the wheel; I committed to making the fastest progress possible. Doing otherwise would have been like a Formula One driver pulling into a pit stop and changing his own tires. The same holds true for you. When you have a process and a coach you believe in and trust, your growth is accelerated by a minimum factor of five times your investment.

But all processes arrive at a "tell the truth" moment. If you are in the insurance industry and your sales manager tells you that they have successfully used the Ben Feldman selling system and sold $100 million of insurance themselves—and that they've successfully shared it with 250 agents who have doubled their revenue every twenty-four months—would you follow the system without deviation?

Remember the 80/20 rule we discussed in chapter 5. Only 20 percent of agents will pursue bold goals, while 80 percent will not. A process is only as good as the link between it and your individual standards. All too often, we set standards that are too low. Ben Feldman's process led to greatness for

him because he always set high expectations for himself—
and then met them.

SET HIGH STANDARDS

What are the standards to which you hold yourself? This is
a vitally important question, because your standards impact
your team, your family, and your results. As one high-profile
business mogul once said: "The quality of a leader is reflected
in the standards they set for themselves." What standards
have you set for yourself in your personal and professional
lives? What are the non-negotiable expectations you have of
yourself? And do you have a process in place for being accountable to your standards?

There are five primary reasons why you should set high
standards for yourself: they lead to higher performance; they
encourage role modeling; they help you to learn and grow;
they attract the talent of others to your endeavor; and they
give you a competitive advantage. They also help you to accomplish more, and to be happier and more effective. Let's
look at how these factors can contribute to your ability to
pursue the impossible.

Higher Performance
We all experience higher performance when we set high
standards for ourselves. Quite simply, if you increase a given
standard by 25 percent, you're likely to experience a 25 percent improved result (or something close to that) because
you've created a new benchmark, a new target. Bannister
broke the four-minute mile because that was the standard he set for himself. It wasn't until after he had broken

that long-standing record that three other runners broke through the same barrier. New benchmarks always increase performance.

Role Modeling

As a leader, you are a role model. Your behavior is continually communicating what's expected of team members. It shapes the culture and drives the behaviors that others deem appropriate for themselves. It determines how they treat their customers.

If you set low standards for yourself, you can never hold your team to a higher standard. When you act as a role model for others, you also call for higher levels of accountability—not only for yourself, but for your team as well. Can you become the avatar or role model for the standards you hold inviolable? Yes!

Learning and Growth

When you raise your standards to a level you're unsure how to accomplish, you naturally reach outside of your current knowledge base and skills to ask for help and get suggestions for improvement. This fosters a culture of learning and encourages innovation and growth—not only for individual leaders, but for all teams and employees.

Pursuing learning and growth doesn't mean chasing after perfection. You don't have to get it right all the time. You just have to aspire to being better. You have to be willing to experiment and take risks in order to learn faster than your competition or those around you. Learning faster than your competitors gives you a distinctly competitive advantage.

Attracting Talent

In an economy where knowledge workers are highly sought, having high standards acts as a dog whistle that attracts the brightest and best talent to your team. If you set low standards, they will act as a turn-off for the superior candidates you want to recruit. High standards attract people with high standards of their own. If the talent you want to recruit is in the top 20 percent of performers, high standards are not an option; they are a requirement.

Competitive Advantage

As we saw above, setting high standards gives you a competitive advantage. The world of work today is incredibly competitive. There's not an industry that doesn't have a competitor seeking to disrupt or reinvent their entire sector. Competition is fierce, and if you and your organization want to have a competitive edge with customers, you have to become the industry standard-bearer that others want to emulate.

Why? Because, your competition is already raising their own standards. If you don't raise yours, you become less competitive and may lose your star customers. Or you may be pressured to lower your fees and become more of a vendor, as opposed to a strategic partner.

THE FOUR HORSEMEN OF THE APOCOLYPSE

If you agree with the five reasons given above, it should be clear to you that, at some point, you'll have to do battle with those in your organization who are content with living a

lukewarm and half-lived life. Stephen Pressfield wrote eloquently about this in his seminal book *The War of Art*.[41]
The moment you start to believe in achieving bold goals and
making bold moves toward them, the four horsemen of the
apocolypse come calling—inertia, ignorance, inexperience,
and indifference. Understanding these barriers will prepare
you for the next chapter, which deals with the inconvenient
truths we are reluctant to express and reluctant to hear.

Inertia

The result of inertia is doing what you've always done in the
past and resisting change. But pursuing bold goals requires
being someone who wants to make a difference and isn't
afraid to pursue activities that lead to change. Even if what
you're doing today is great, what you'll do two years from
now to achieve greatness will be very different from what
you're doing now. As we saw in the last chapter, to move forward, you have to move outside of your comfort zone. And
when you're tired, overworked, and have a to-do list as long
as the Brooklyn Bridge, that's very hard to do. Maintaining
the status quo becomes like a siren song.

Every single one of my clients is overscheduled when we
start our work together. The complaints I hear most are: I
want my life back; I want to do great work, but I don't have
the time to be innovative; I want to advance in my career
and be successful, but when I'm stuck in back-to-back meetings for ten hours straight, that's impossible. So I tell clients
up front that our first job is to free up 15 percent of their
schedules as a starting point. Some fight me, because I am
ruthless with their calendars, paring down what needs to get

scheduled and showing them how to manage their boards' or bosses' expectations.

The antidote to inertia is falling in love with one idea that can make your company significantly better at doing what it does and create more fun and flow. In turn, this creates more success for you as a leader. I help leaders remove every single thought and action that are not essential to and supportive of the one idea or activity that's a game-changer for them. One of the most rewarding parts of my job is hearing high-level executives say: "I never thought it was possible to live and lead like this. I have my life back and I've never felt so liberated." That's when I know that they have fought inertia and won.

Ignorance

The word "ignorance" has an understandably negative connotation. You'd never call an employee ignorant—at least, I certainly hope you wouldn't! But many of my clients are ignorant of the need to slow down and focus in order to go faster. Technology executives and entrepreneurs are usually brilliant when it comes to technical issues; yet they tend to be bound to electronic devices that are continually giving them dopamine hits and isolating them from other, more important issues.

These leaders are not broken, nor are they Neanderthals dragging their knuckles on the ground. They're smart, but they're smart about all things other than what's required to create the organizational transformation they so desperately want. They're ignorant about people and relationships, and about deep flow and the focus side of leadership.

Inexperience

When I use the word "inexperience" here, I'm not referring
to the capabilities of leaders, but rather to leadership talents
and skills that need to be developed. To achieve bold goals,
leaders and teams must continually ask themselves what new
experiences and education they need to do great work. Is
there one idea that has fired up the team? Where is the team
being successful and where are they experiencing setbacks?
Do they have an outside perspective or are they just breath-
ing their own exhaust?

Indifference

Indifference is a trait that, unfortunately, is not in short supply these days. Moreover, although the first three obstacles
described here can be addressed by planning and action,
indifference is nearly impossible to overcome. Over two days,
I had two customer-service representatives express zero interest in helping me with a recent purchase I had made at one
of my favorite clothing stores. I had bought some shirts that
I liked and I wanted to know when they would be back in
stock so I could buy another. The employee told me to keep
checking the store's website. When I asked if there was an
easier way to get the information, or if I could receive a no-
tification of some kind, he simply said "no." When I asked
if my only recourse was to return the purchase and shop
elsewhere, he answered "yes."

Now, my request didn't seem outlandish to me, but ap-
parently it did to the employee. I did not want to return my
purchase. I just wanted to know when the item would be
available. When the employee pulled up my order, he said

(and I'm quoting here): "I see you've placed ten orders in the last two years." This should have clearly indicated to him that I was probably a good customer. And he still didn't care if I took my business elsewhere. Will I shop there again? Not likely. This exchange left a bad taste in my mouth and tarnished the company's brand for me.

I'm not sure what the manager of that customer-service team had planted in the fertile soil of this employee's imagination, but it wasn't a love of customers or a love of helping them feel special. It was indifference.

QUESTIONS

Ask yourself these questions to determine whether you are successfully pursuing the impossible and combatting the four horsemen.

- What do you hear others call impossible that you know to be possible for you and your team?
- The last time you accomplished what others thought was an impossible objective, what did you and your team commit to doing differently thereafter?
- Which of the five reasons to raise your standards is most compelling for you? Why?
- Which of the four horseman are you currently battling? Who is winning?

In the next chapter, we'll examine why difficult conversations about greatness often fail to take place and how speaking the unspoken can increase performance and enhance results.

CHAPTER 19

Speaking the Unspoken

If I could only give three words of advice, they would be, "Tell the truth." If I got three more words, I'd add, "All the time."

RANDY PAUSCH

To pursue a strategy of living boldly, you have to be willing to bring unspoken truths out into the open. One conversation can change the trajectory of your life. It can take you from living in fear to living a life of greatness. One purposeful and intentional conversation holds the potential to achieve a transformation in our beliefs, our perceptions, and, ultimately, in our capacity for boldness.

I've built my career around helping leaders and teams change their behavior—one of the hardest things they will ever do. One of my clients, a technology executive, told me that my superpower (I didn't know I had one!) was that I brought the unspoken out into the open and, by doing so, created a pathway for people to live life more fully. I was grateful for his comment, because I know that speaking the unspoken in a harried and busy world is a bold act.

Our conversations today tend to be more transactional than transformational. I see many people in organizations engaging in what I call "bus-stop" conversations—exchanges that remain on a surface level and don't reach down to the things that are important, meaningful, and, most important, bold. LeBron James and other world-class athletes are not interested in superficial or transactional conversations. They're committed to exchanges that change their individual and team performance. They are heat-seeking missiles for insights and wisdom about getting better, even if only by 1 percent each day.

MISSING THE BUS

Living boldly yourself or helping others to live boldly doesn't afford you the luxury of having bus-stop conversations. Meaningful dialogue is required to know what's working and what's not. These exchanges go deeper and bring out the best in the people involved. In our overscheduled and overworked world of work, however, bus-stop conversations have become the norm and are hardwired into our way of thinking and leading. When we sacrifice the ability to bring the unspoken out into the open, we "miss the bus," so to speak. We lose access to the wisdom, insights, and potential of those with whom we work.

The 1992 movie *A Few Good Men* is a great example of bringing the unspoken out into the open. In it, an old-school marine officer is accused of ordering the hazing of a marine to punish him for demonstrating inferior character and commitment. The plot revolves around whether the officer was responsible for the death of the hazed marine. The officer, obviously, wants to keep facts hidden; the lawyer wants to bring the truth out into the open. As in most courtroom dramas, there's a pivotal moment when the lawyer confronts the officer and demands that he tell the truth. When pressed, the officer explodes with disdain and indignation: "You want to know the truth? You can't handle the truth!"

This powerful scene reflects the consequences of speaking the unspoken in our professional and personal lives. The unspoken is left unspoken for a reason. We want to protect ourselves from being vulnerable. We want to avoid accountability for our actions. We want to disparage those who ask us to be truthful. The officer is motivated by a desire to avoid the consequences of his actions. The lawyer wants to hold him accountable. And neither one respects the other or his motives.

9:00 TO 5:00 TRUTH

Writer Hunter S. Thompson once quipped: "I have a theory that the truth is never told during the nine-to-five hours."[42] And there's a reason why the truth is so hard to find at work. It's not that people feel a greater desire to lie in the workplace. It's because there's no payoff for telling the truth if the goals or expectations on teams are misaligned.

A client who is a vice president of human resources had some bad news to share with her CEO. He was a brilliant technology leader, but lacked the relationship skills to lead his company of fifty people. She was hearing weekly questions and concerns about his being dismissive and nonresponsive, and of him communicating a message that he was superior to everyone else, and everyone else should be grateful to have a job. She knew the CEO personally and wanted to help him be successful. But she was hesitant to confront him for fear of being dismissed as a human resources "softy." She wanted to be seen as an intelligent strategic partner.

We mapped out a process that positioned the soft side of leadership and team effectiveness in a strategic and data-driven manner. I encouraged her to tell him the truth, and to acknowledge that her job is to tell executives what they need to hear in a way they can hear it. When she pulled the trigger and shared everything she wanted to tell the CEO, she told me: "I was 100 percent successful in getting his attention and 80 percent successful in getting him to listen to suggestions for action. But I wasn't successful in getting him to agree to do anything about the problem."

This executive's experience highlights a key point made by Dan Sullivan: "All progress starts with telling the truth."[43] The truth that needs to be brought out into the open in the world of work is not the absolute truth about the origins of the universe. It's the truth about behavior, and whether it's helpful or hurtful to achieving a goal or objective. Anyone in a leadership or coaching role has an obligation to tell people the truth—what they need to hear—in a way they can actually hear it. We do so because speaking the unspoken is a bold move. It has the potential to change the trajectory of an employee's or customer's life.

TRUTH-TELLERS AND TRUTH-LISTENERS

To be a truth-teller, you must be a "truth-listener." Most of us have experienced a moment of truth-telling that was necessary to address the gap between where employees currently are and where they need to be. But the last time someone had to tell you the unvarnished truth about your own behavior, how did you respond?

Deryck was a young senior vice president who was smart, driven, and a high-potential young leader. The problem was that he didn't listen to others' observations and feedback. He rebuffed suggestions for improvement from his boss and from the COO, and he communicated in ways that left others frustrated and unwilling to work with him.

Deryck was placed on a performance improvement plan (PIP). The company thought highly enough of him that they were willing to invest in a coach if he were willing to work to map out a path to improve. As the coach in question, I had two key questions to answer: Was Deryck coachable and open to suggestions? And did Deryck believe a coach could help him improve his leadership? When Deryck and I met online, we exchanged pleasantries and, within ten minutes, I experienced the same behaviors that had prompted the COO to request my help.

When I asked him if he undertood that his employment might be in jeopardy if his issues were not addressed successfully, he responded: "Yes, but . . ." Yes, but it wasn't his fault if other people were intimidated by him, or if their self-confidence was not as high as his. When I asked if he ever dismissed different perspectives because he believed his own was superior to theirs, he answered: "Yes, but . . ." Yes, but he often had a clearer and more effective understanding than others. When I asked about people being frustrated with his communication style and not wanting to work with him, he replied: "Yes, but . . ." Yes, but his team was loyal to him and were working hard. "I don't have a problem with my team," he complained, "so I don't understand the problem."

The problem, as you can see, is that Deryck, even when faced with the prospect of losing his job, continued to respond to my questions or observations with a "Yes, but . . ." attitude. His first instinct was to make excuses and minimize the COO's concerns. I told him that, if he did this with his stakeholders and boss, it would be a career-limiting move.

Every successful coaching relationship is built on mutual trust and respect. For Deryck and me to partner on his success, I needed to speak the unspoken. And more important, he needed to *listen*. Only then could progress be made.

So I told him that I myself was experiencing the behaviors about which others were complaining. He replied with another "Yes, but . . ." At that point, I told him that I was probably not the best coach for him and that he needed to find an alternative. When he asked me why, I said: "Because you're not a good listener." I told him that I thought that, no matter what I said, he would refute it or try to justify his behavior. I explained to him that he thought his views were always right and dismissed others' perspectives, and intellectualized strategically important conversations, like the one about his own employment with the organization. "If we were to work together," I said, "we would just be running around in circles and wouldn't make any progress. That's a waste of my time and yours, and a waste of company resources."

After a few moments, Deryck told me that his wife had said almost the same thing to him as he left the house that morning. At that moment, something shifted dramatically in his attitude and he showed a vulnerability not evident before. When the unspoken came out into the open and Deryck actually listened, our conversation ceased being a bus-stop conversation and became transformational.

The event that changed everything for Deryck was having an outsider tell him what he needed to hear in a way that he could hear it. What made him want to improve was recognizing the truth of what had previously been left unspoken.

Over the next four months, Deryck worked hard at improving and reaped significant rewards for himself and his company in the process. His new level of clarity and new ways of communicating changed the trajectory of his career as a leader.

THE KEYS TO TRUTH-TELLING

Learning how to speak the unspoken requires that you understand and implement three simple strategies: be clear, be curious, and be kind. Let's look at each one of these to see how it can contribute to an atmosphere of truth-telling in the workplace—and in your personal life as well.

Be Clear
In my work, I often hear team members complain about how unclear their leaders' expectations are. The simple act

of getting clear is a bold move, and an accelerator of performance. Trying to lead without clarity is like driving with one
foot on the accelerator and one foot on the brake.

Clear expectations are essential to living boldly. If others
are to meet your expectations, they must be clear on the
specific behaviors or results expected of them. If these expectations are unclear, they may work hard and do an excellent
job achieving a result you didn't really want.

In addition to being clear, expectations must be understood. This involves telling others the why, what, how, when,
where, and who involved in the goal. Clear goals typically
express a desired outcome as well as a current state, and a
reason for wanting to close the gap between the two. They
must also be specific and concrete. They must isolate the
desired behaviors and the corresponding results sought in
order to close the gap between the current and future states.
And this means they must be accompanied by clear metrics
and a corresponding time frame.

Expectations also need to be relevant to the business. They
can be challenging and may represent a "raising of the bar,"
but team members have to be confident that they can succeed and understand why it's important to do so. If relevant
context and confidence are missing, you may see heads nod-
ding, but the expectation may never be realized within the
desired metrics or timeframe.

A vital last step in being clear is to confirm what's been
discussed and agreed upon. Ask others to communicate their
understanding of the situation or expectation—their role in
accomplishing it and the results for which they're responsible. If they can't, they cannot truly commit to it. When they
get clear about expectations, 90 percent of people will work

diligently to fulfill these commitments. This clarity builds trust and respect, and preserves personal dignity. The more clear you are, the more clear others will be about their commitments. This can help you achieve your most important priorities much faster.

Be Curious

When a deadline is missed or an expectation goes unmet, be curious. This can help you bring the unspoken out into the open. If you approach the conversation with hopes of finding fault and laying blame, however, you'll push people into a corner and lose access to their insights or wisdom.

When discussing an expectation that has gone unmet, I use words like "curious" and "confused" to open the conversation: "I'm curious. When you and I spoke about the ABC project, my understanding was that we would accomplish D, E, and F by June 30, 2024. I see we aren't going to meet that deadline, even though we both expected that would happen. What insights or perspective do you have about the delay that I may not be considering?"

The important thing to remember here is your *tone of voice*. If you ask this question with an edge to it or in anger, you'll get nowhere. But if you are genuinely and sincerely concerned about the gap between expectations and results and want to figure out why it occurred, use the words "curious" or "confused" when you ask for clarification.

Be Kind

Nine times out of ten, when a deadline is missed or an expectation goes unmet, there's some form of misunderstanding as to what was expected. Think of these misunderstandings as a surefire way to keep you from bringing out the very best in others. If you want to create a culture of bold moves and growth, remember the word "agape" that we discussed in Part I.

If you seek the highest and best for yourself and those you work and live with, be kind to them. I'm not suggesting that you not hold others accountable if they repeatedly drop the ball and don't fulfill their commitments. On the contrary, I believe that the kind thing to do in that situation is to have a clear, candid, and considerate conversation about underperformance.

If you're clear, curious, and kind, your discomfort in these conversations will go down, and the results you achieve will go up.

QUESTIONS

Here are some questions to consider when rating your own truth-telling—and truth-listening—skills.

- On a scale of one to ten, how would you rate your truth-telling skills about your impact on others?
- Based on your answer to the first question, what are you most afraid of learning about yourself professionally?
- Name one conversation in which you haven't spoken the truth to a powerful person. What is the impact on you and on the other person of your not being truthful?
- Being ruthlessly honest with yourself, what four words would you use to best describe you and your your capacity for telling and hearing the truth?

- If your direct reports were ruthlessly honest with you, what four words would they use to describe you and your capacity for telling and hearing the truth?

The quote that opened this chapter stressed how important it is to tell the truth all the time—even in situations pervaded by deceit. The deceit that can defeat you as a leader is the deceit of those who have a high capacity to deceive themselves as to their strengths and blind spots. But one conversation can change that. What bold truth-telling conversation are you most in need of having?

In the final chapter, I'll show you how implementing the strategies we've discussed in Part III can help you stretch toward greatness.

CHAPTER 20

Living into Greatness

*Greatness comes by doing a few small and smart things
each and every day. Comes from taking little steps,
consistently. Comes from making a few small chips
against everything in your professional and personal
life that is ordinary, so that a day eventually arrives
when all that's left is The Extraordinary.*

ROBIN S. SHARMA

If you're like the majority of my clients, you're thinking
about ways to implement the ideas we've discussed in this
book and apply them to your own leadership. You're primed
and ready to achieve bold and real-world results. The Stretch
100 Project is a plan that can help you do just that.

The Stretch 100 Project outlines a process for creating and
completing passionate and enthusiastic projects that matter
most to the people who matter most to you—and to do so in
significantly shorter periods of time. Exploring this plan will
help you integrate the insights presented in this book and
stretch you to apply them rapidly and passionately.

But let's be clear. There are very few things that are vitally important to your success. Remember the 80/20 rule (see chapter 5). Twenty percent of your activities create 80 percent of your results. The rest of your efforts are trivial. These activities may pay the bills, but they can drastically reduce your effectiveness, your success, and your satisfaction and enjoyment at work. On the other hand, knowing and working from your critical 20 percent is a bold move that can help you live into greatness.

THE STRETCH 100 PROJECT

I developed the Stretch 100 Project to help leaders deliver a concise, compressed, and value-creating experience for themselves and their customers. The project relies on four key principles: accelerated learning, greater customer intimacy, clearly articulated value, and increased success and satisfaction. Let's look at each one of these more closely.

Accelerated Learning

My clients aspire to achieve a level of excellence and are drawn to accomplishing results similar to those of Ben Feldman (see chapter 18). With habit-stacking—building new habits by identifying a current habit, then "stacking" your new behavior on top of it—and intentionality, you can become 100 percent better at one leadership skill within 100 days. This doesn't mean you will achieve greatness in 100 days. Rather it means that you will have laid the neural pathways for the process of achieving greatness in your chosen field.

You can accelerate your learning by compressing the time-frame. Knowing you have only 100 days to complete your project can instill a intrinsic sense of urgency and make you more willing to apply what you've learned in real time. This creates a greater sense of urgency and leverage.

Greater Customer Intimacy

If you love your customers, you want to get closer to them and make their lives better. You want to understand their hopes, dreams, and aspirations as clearly as you understand your own. Understanding their strategic objectives, their priorities, and how you can help them is a critical first step in any project. I don't advocate undertaking a project that, although engaging for you, doesn't create any stakeholder value. Creating customer value and intimacy, integrated with your accelerated learning, can generate a win for both you and your customers.

Clearly Articulated Value

The Stretch 100 Project involves conducting a series of client interviews to learn the issues that matter most to your customers. The questions used are geared to isolate what they consider to be their biggest problem and the price attached to that problem. As one of my mentors once told me: "Before you ever become a problem-solver, become a problem-finder." Identifying a problem and knowing its price is an essential first step to creating high value for your clients.

The Stretch 100 Project gives you a process that can help you communicate your brand and your value with clarity and conviction, and convert it into behaviorally explicit actions that increase your reputation.

Increased Success and Satisfaction

Too many projects are cumbersome and lumbering. They involve people who don't love their work or what they do—people who are living lukewarm lives. They are disinterested in creating bold results for their stakeholders. Projects with people like this are a drain on the success and satisfaction of all involved.

The Stretch 100 Project provides a blueprint for producing greater success and satisfaction, while also completing value-enhancing and transformational work. These projects are designed to perform work that matters and delights your customers, and create outcomes that make them feel as if they're in a significantly better position for having done the work. This puts a bounce in your step and excites and engages you by challenging your current skills and providing you with the autonomy, clear goals, and intrinsic rewards that make the project a big win for all involved. And perhaps most important, these projects can fulfill your team's and your organization's driving need to increase stakeholder value.

Engaging in a Stretch 100 project creates a framework in which you and your stakeholders can see possibilities that others don't see. In his book *The Art of Possibility*, Benjamin Zander tells of a shoe factory that sent two marketing scouts to a region in Africa to study the prospects for expanding its business. One sent back a telegram that said: "Situation hopeless. STOP. No one wears shoes." The other sent one that read: "Glorious business opportunity. STOP. They have no shoes."[44] To one marketing executive, all of the evidence pointed to hopelessness. To the other, the same conditions pointed to terrific opportunities.

The principles presented throughout this book position you for greater success when implementing a Stretch 100 project. They help you push the boundaries of what increased speed to success looks like. As Mario Andretti once said: "If everything feels like it's under control, you're simply not going fast enough."

FULL SPEED AHEAD

As the name suggests, The Stretch 100 Project is based on the number 100.

- 100% enthusiasm: The project is a labor of love for you.
- 100% commitment: You're committed to learning, growing, and pursuing boldness.
- 100% focus: You remove all distractions and give 80 percent of your focus and attention to the 20 percent of your highest-value activities.
- 100 days: You complete the project in seventy-two business days—or 100 calendar days.

To create this shift in perspective, the strategy is divided into three phases that are aligned with the principles expressed in this book: investigation, inspiration, and implementation.

In the investigation phase, you conduct stakeholder interviews using a framework for identifying their highest priorities, listening deeply, then finding a problem and putting a price tag on it. The inspiration phase aligns what you learned in your investigation with one or two goals that excite you the most—what captures or creates the most shareholder value—and clarifies the problem you're deeply committed to solving in 100 days. The implementation phase outlines a weekly process for reviewing your progress on your commitments, your milestones, and your next steps—all while having fun.

Let's get started.

INVESTIGATION PHASE

In the investigation phase, your goal is to identify the five or ten stakeholders or customers that matter most to you. These are the individuals to whom you seek to deliver the greatest value. These are also individuals about whom you care deeply. You desire significant success for them and seek to understand them and their situations. You also want them to perceive you as a true strategic partner and not as a vendor.

It's important to note that some of these stakeholders may produce significant amounts of revenue for you. So by extension, they're vitally important to you and your business. That level of contribution to your financial results makes your Stretch 100 project all the more important.

The most important thing in this first step is that you don't simply want to know what is right for your stakeholders intellectually. You want to hear first-hand what's important to them because they, as individuals, are important. They're not simply a vehicle for sending money your way.

After you have identified five to ten stakeholders, schedule a forty-five to sixty-minute interview with each one. In these interviews, which are directly linked to the principles presented in Part II, pay special attention to what you learned in chapters 7 (embracing humble swagger) and 10 (cultivating passion). Make sure you bring these two characteristics into the interview.

Below are questions I suggest you ask. I formulated these questions based on my own interpretation of a framework developed by Tommy Schaff—one of the most masterful client-engagement experts I know. He calls the framework STORY, because it is grounded in five key elements: situation, target, obstacles, responses, and yield.[45] This questioning framework has dramatically changed the way I engage with my clients, and I believe it will do the same for your Stretch 100 project as well.

And most important, within a day of conducting the interviews, send a summary to your clients in what is called an "artifact." This will accomplish two things. It will confirm for your stakeholders that you understood them and, perhaps more important, it will give you a touch point with your customers that they've never had before. This can take you one step closer to creating customer delight, and differentiation.

Stakeholder Interview Questions
Current situation:
- What is the most important strategic priority you have today?
- Why is that important to you?

- What are the outcomes you're currently getting in your strategic priorities?
- Is that exceeding expectations, hitting the mark, or missing benchmarks where you need/want to be?

Target situation:
- Let's pretend it's three years from now. What you seek is now working and exceeding all metrics to which you committed. What will this deliver for you and the organization?
- What are the milestones that are most important in the future?
- How will you measure these?

Obstacles and challenges:
- What is stopping you from closing the gap between where you are and where you want to be?
- Anything else?

Responses tried:
- In what ways have you tried to resolve these obstacles?
- How did that work?
- Anything else?

Yield or impact:
- Consider what would happen if you did nothing. What would the situation be like in your area in three years?
- What problems will accumulate?
- Which of your goals will not be met?
- What will it cost the company?

- Besides loss of revenue, what else will happen?
- In what timeframe do these objectives need to be accomplished?
- How important is this to you personally?
- Is there anyone else who needs to be involved?

Once your stakeholders have answered these questions, you are ready to move on to the inspiration phase.

INSPIRATION PHASE

After completing your stakeholder interviews, begin to focus on three areas of questions: What results will serve your stakeholders best? What metrics will you use to keep your stakeholders and yourself excited and engaged? What bold value can you create in 100 days?

Review your client's artifact and isolate your answers to the following questions. It's vitally important when it comes to living and leading boldly that you reject vague or general answers to the questions that follow. You must know with clarity and specificity what are the most important results you want to achieve, what results are most closely aligned with your leadership purpose, and what results are aligned with your greatest strengths to create the best results.

You *do not* have to answer all of these questions. Use them solely as a catalyst to help you think creatively about the most important results you heard from your stakeholders. After you complete this phase, you'll be better able to discuss ideas for projects with your stakeholders and gain the green light to move forward.

Results Clarification

- What conditions would you love to see improve around your department, team, or organization?
- Ideally, in a world without any barriers, what would you like to accomplish?
- What single thing could you do to make your organization experience a positive difference that would be extraordinary?
- How can your customers be better served?
- What can you do that would leave your boss saying: "I love working with you"?
- What can make your employees' lives significantly easier?
- What precise aspects of your work are most troubling to you? What keeps you up at night?
- If you had to set priorities now that would have a significant positive impact on your team or organization, what three things must be accomplished?
- What is the most important result your organization is pursuing regarding key metrics? Are there ways you can help achieve them?
- What market share/profitability/productivity improvement does your organization expect?
- How are you evaluated or measured in your current role?

Measures of Success

These questions can help you identify which of your project ideas has the strongest prospect of being successful. Consider how you'll know you've accomplished this objective.

- What is acceptable improvement and ideal improvement for each of your project ideas? Does one set of improvements excite you more than another?
- How will the environment/culture/structure be improved for each of your project ideas?
- What will the impact be on your key metrics?
- What form will the information need to take in order for it to be helpful?
- Do you have the right information from customers/vendors/employees/bosses to know whether you've been successful?
- How frequently will you need to assess progress, and how will you do it?
- How will you be able to prove your success to others?

Value Contribution

Answer these questions after you have identified two or three projects that you believe can provide value to your team or organization, but before discussing this with your boss.

- What if you do nothing? What will the impact be?
- What if your project fails?
- What does this mean to you personally?
- What would the difference be for the organization/customers/employees if you were supremely successful?
- How will this project affect performance?
- How will this affect image/morale/safety/reputation?
- What would the effect be on productivity/profitability/market share?
- What is this now costing you annually?
- What is the impact on key metrics?

Your Personal Contribution to Value Creation

- Why you? Can any employee do this, or do you have special attributes?
- Why now? Is the timing particularly urgent or sensitive?
- Why in this manner? Is there some aspect of the methodologies or relationships that is key at the moment?
- What's unique about your relationship to the parties involved? Do you have a level of trust that can help you be successful?
- What's your unique value-added? To what extent can you "guarantee" success and exceed your constituents' expectations?

Identify up to three projects that you believe are important. Consider what value they provide and why you should invest time in them. Once you have this information, you are ready to identify the people necessary for your success, as well as the opposing and promoting forces of success.

Talent Magnetism

- Who should be involved in your project?
- Who represents the best thinking, best attitude, most experience, greatest passion, etc. for your project, and who can bring the most energy and creativity?

Opposing Barriers and Promoting Forces

- What are the barriers to a satisfying and successful completion of your project? Brainstorm the longest list possible.
- What are the helpful forces that can secure a satisfying and successful completion of your project?

IMPLEMENTATION PHASE

Shifting into the implementation phase is the most important part of a Stretch 100 project. Remember, you're not accomplishing an entire project in 100 days. You're taking one smaller, but valuable, aspect of a project and accomplishing it in 100 days. The goal is to align what you love doing at work with the guiding principles for leading boldly and integrating them into how you live and work today. You're not seeking perfection; you're seeking progress, growth, learning, and experimentation. You're seeking to embrace the principles you learned in Part II in the context of a project that matters to you and your stakeholders.

Weekly Process Reviews

As the name implies, these reviews indicate your progress from one week to the next. They ensure that you have clear expectations and statements of accomplishment from week to week. That means laying out the three tasks or objectives you'll accomplish over the next five business days and naming where you'll be accountable, along with metrics attached to each deliverable. So far, nothing here is new.

What's different is that you also integrate the eight principles from Part II as ways of doing business. You specifically discuss what you've learned and your leadership growth as it relates to your project. In these meetings, you make a weekly commitment or promise about what you'll accomplish the following week.

Another differentiating aspect of a Stretch 100 project is that you invite stakeholders to observe or participate in these meetings. By doing so, you invite them into the details of the project and share your progress, thereby providing a model for the second characteristic discussed in Part II—accountability. Your weekly review demonstrates a full measure of collaboration and should include clear definitions of what excellence and boldness look like.

In these reviews, you should have zero tolerance for violations of the principles discussed in Part II. While being successful and accomplishing bold results at work are important, it's equally important to treat people in ways that build trust and respect, and preserve personal dignity.

The eight traits and characteristics in Part II are designed to create an environment where people can do their very best when the culture tries to bring out the worst in them. Remember, although adherence to all these guiding principles is important, the very first principle is *humility*. These traits and characteristics are about progress, not perfection. But it's important to remember that, when and if someone intentionally and repeatedly violates any of the principles, their behavior needs to be addressed swiftly and directly.

Use radical candor. Remember that integrity is one of the eight guiding principles. The candor that's required to lead boldly leverages humility, accountability, the pursuit of excellence, and integrity. If you commit to doing something, then you have to pull out all the stops and make sure you accomplish your tasks. The traits and characteristics in Part II guide your behavior and build a level of trust and respect that allows for radical candor. They are not a stick, however, with which to hit people over the head. They are guidelines for how to build a healthy and vibrant culture.

And be sure to have fun. Frankly, without fun, work becomes nothing more than crawling on our bellies through enemy territory with bullets flying over our heads. No one wants to work in that environment and, if they do, they will not be doing their very best work. Whatever you do, care for the hearts and minds of the people who work with you and help them flourish at work. Then and only then will they bring their very best selves to work and accomplish bold results.

QUESTIONS

When you are ready to stretch toward greatness, ask yourself these questions:

- What is the one project I would love to do?
- What impact would that project have, and does it excite me just thinking about it?
- Am I willing to challenge my assumptions about time, energy, and focus to achieve the best result?
- Will any of these projects require new learning and growth on my part? Which one will require the greatest growth?
- How will I solicit the talent needed to be successful?
- Which barrier do I want to tackle first? Where can I build success, gain momentum, and build enthusiasm?
- What are the promoting forces I'll harness to be successful?

Once you have these answers, schedule a meeting to outline your project options with your stakeholders. Share the results you envision with them and discuss the barriers you want to break down. Then decide when you will launch your project.

Following the Stretch 100 plan can help you implement all the insights that you have gained in this book and set you on the path to personal and professional greatness.

And as you embark on that journey, remember to *live boldly*!

CONCLUSION:
BEWARE THE BLACK DOG

I set out on the journey of living boldly for my own well-being. For what could have been labeled as "way too long," I had lived in fear. During those years, I was never at my best, nor was I doing my best for the people who mattered most to me—my family, my friends, my clients, or my community. My mother called the fear I was experiencing "the black dog." When the black dog visited, I was difficult to live with—intensely negative, impatient, and with a very hard edge to me.

In early 2003, the black dog set up shop in my head, resulting in a depressive episode that lasted three months. I had never experienced this level of darkness for that long. I became nearly immobile, nonresponsive, and disinterested in the basics of daily life. I never reached the point of wanting to take my life, but I did feel as if I no longer had a desire to live. With the love and support of my wife, a good friend, and a caring and insightful physician, I came out of that dark place. But the experience taught me that, while there are biochemical, physiological, and psychological factors that influence depression, there are also rituals and practices that can improve our mental health and well-being.

This led me to a deeper appreciation and understanding of how loving deeply opened a gateway to a whole host of possibilities that I couldn't see before. I learned how to deepen my understanding of the black dog, reframe my situation and responses to it, and apply what I was learning more behaviorally. Most important, I found myself sharing my insights with unbridled enthusiasm. In some ways, this book is the culmination of that experience.

My own experience learning as much as I could about something I dearly love—human potential and performance—convinced me that my next best step was to share with you what I've learned and, in turn, taught to others who were also committed to converting their lives of fear, worry, or trepidation into lives lived boldly. And I am grateful to you for having invested your most precious commodity—your time—in reading a book about loving deeply, learning daily, and living boldly.

Throughout this book, I have asked you to answer bold questions. You may not have answered them all, but I hope that each of them contained a provocative idea—a springboard that will help you take the ideas about which you've read and convert them into actions that can help you live and lead boldly.

The questions in Part I teach you that, when you live without an agape type of love, you confine yourself to a life of self-referential attachment. When this happens, you want what you want, and your actions are rooted in filling your own needs and desires regardless of how they impact others. At work, you become transactional and the people you work with grow distrustful of your motives and become protective and standoffish. This presents a significant risk that affects your relationships as well as your performance and satisfaction at work.

The questions in Part II emphasize eight key traits that you need to cultivate before you can move toward greatness. They help demonstrate how you engage with challenges—as threats to be avoided, or as opportunities for greater insight and wisdom. Do you give up easily when faced with obstacles? Or do you persist until you achieve a successful completion? Do you see the effort required for success as frivolous or fruitless? Or do you see it as a pathway to greatness? Do you ignore criticism? Or do you see it as a catalyst for learning? Do you see the success of others as a threat, or as an inspiration?

The questions in Part III, if answered intellectually but not internalized, can leave you stuck in neutral—or with one foot firmly on the brake rather than on the accelerator. This leads to a lukewarm and timid life filled with regret—not for the things you've done, but for what you neglected to do out of fear and uncertainty. When regret for your unrealized potential envelops you, so does the dissatisfaction of knowing that you did not pursue your very best.

If you aspire to achieve personal or professional greatness for yourself, as well as enable greatness in others, this book can act as your coach. My most sincere dream for you is that you love deeply all the people who matter most to you, that you embrace and embody the eight characteristics of healthy cultures and successful leaders, and that you commit to living a life of boldness. I hope that, in some small way, this will make your life more rewarding and fulfilling, and that you will in turn do the same for others.

ENDNOTES

INTRODUCTION

1. S. Farber, *Love Is Just Damn Good Business*, (New York: McGraw Hill, 2019).

CHAPTER 2

2. Aaron Armstrong (n.d.), "What C. S. Lewis wrote is more powerful than what he didn't," *artofmanliness.com*.

3. D. Lavinsky, "The Secret to Success in Business and Life," *growthink.com*.

CHAPTER 3

4. Bob Rotella, *How Champions Think*, (New York: Simon & Schuster, 2016), p. 4.

5. Dan Sullivan, "Best Career Advice: 10 Secrets to Success for Today's Entrepreneur," *resources.strategiccoach.com*.

6. William Hutchinson Murray, *The Scottish Himalayan Expedition*, (London: J. M. Dent and Company, 1951).

CHAPTER 4

7. J. G. Weigel (2012), "The Truelove by David Whyte," *high-road-artist.com*.

CHAPTER 5

8. M. Popova (n.d.). "The Truelove: Poet and Philosopher David Whyte on Reaching beyond Our Limiting Beliefs," *themarginalian.org*.

9. Ibid.

CHAPTER 7

10. R. Warren, *The Purpose Driven Life* (Grand Rapids, MI: Zondervan, 2012).

11. J. Collins, *Good to Great* (HarperAudio, 2010).

12. James M. Kouzes and Barry Z. Posner, *The Leadership Challenge*, 6th ed. (Hoboken, NJ: Josey-Bass, 2017).

13. Unsourced. Often attributed to Shaw, but to many others as well.

14. T. Chamorro-Premuzic (2020), "Why Humble Leaders Are Rare," *forbes.com*.

15. "Become a World-Class Executive Coach," *mgscc.net*.

CHAPTER 9

16. T. J. Peters and R. H. Waterman, *In Search of Excellence: Lessons from America's Best-Run Companies,* (HarperBusiness, 2006).

CHAPTER 10

17. Kaiser Family Foundation, *kff.org*.

18. National Institutes of Health, "Turning Discovery into Health," *nih.gov*; see also *kff.org* and "COVID Health," *covid19.nih.gov*.

19. "Peter Drucker on Marketing," *forbes.com*.

CHAPTER 11

20. A. Lembke, *Dopamine Nation: Finding Balance in the Age of Indulgence*, (New York: Dutton, 2021).

21. T. J. Peters and R. H. Waterman, *In Search of Excellence: Lessons from America's Best-Run Companies*, (HarperBusiness, 2006).

22. T. Peters, *Excellence Now: Extreme Humanism*, (Chicago: Networlding Publishing, 2021.

23. The Welcome Conference (July 19, 2018), *Alan Mulally—Working Together* [video], *youtube.com*.

CHAPTER 15

24. C. Tardi (n.d.), "What Is Moore's Law and Is It Still True?" *investopedia.com*.

25. M. Rao, "Be Adaptable: Leadership Lessons from Jack Welch," (*Training*, June 6, 2017).

26. A. Deutschman, "Change or Die," (*Fast Company*, 2005).

27. Deutschman, "Change or Die."

28. *healthsystemtracker.org*.

29. Edward D. Miller, M.D. (n.d.), *hopkinsmedicine.org*.

30. Dean Ornish (n.d.), "The Ornish Reversal Program: Intensive Cardiac Rehabilitation," *ornish.com*.

31. "Peter Robertson," *human-insight.com*.

32. D. G. Thomson, *Blueprint to a Billion: 7 Essentials to Achieve Exponential Growth,* (Hoboken, NJ: Wiley, 2005).

33. "What is growth mindset?" *understood.org.*

34. M. Goldsmith, *What Got You Here Won't Get You There,* (New York: Hachette Books, 2007).

CHAPTER 16

35. "CliftonStrengths Answers, "Who Am I?" *gallup.com*; see also "HIGH 5 Test Review: Does It Unlock Your Superpowers?" *insideoutmastery.com.*

CHAPTER 17

36. "What Is Rational Emotive Behavior Therapy (REBT)?" *verywellmind.com.*

37. "Sports Don't Build Character,*"faithdrivenathlete.org.*

38. L. Dell'Osso, P. Lorenzi, B. Nardi, C. Carmassi, and B. Carpita, (2022), "Post-Traumatic Growth (PTG) in the Frame of Traumatic Experiences," *doi.org.*

39. Hal Hershfield, *Your Future Self,* (New York: Little, Brown Spark, 2023); Benjamin Hardy, *Be Your Future Self Now,* (Carlsbad, CA: Hay House Business, 2022).

CHAPTER 18

40. "Agency History,*"thefeldmanagency.com.*

41. S. Pressfield and S. Coyne, *The War of Art: Break Through the Blocks and Win Your Inner Creative Battles,* (Mission, TX: Black Irish Books, 2012).

CHAPTER 19

42. "Hunter S Thompson: In His Own Words," *theguardian.com.*

43. Dan Sullivan, *10X Is Easier than 2X* [video], *10xtalk.com.*

CHAPTER 20

44. R. S. Zander and B. Zander, *The Art of Possibility: Transforming Professional and Personal Life* (New York: Penguin Books, 2002).

45. T. Schaff (n.d.), "All-Star Virtual Training Camp," *majorleaguesales.com.*

RESOURCES

PRINT RESOURCES

Blane, H. *7 Principles of Transformational Leadership: Create a Mindset of Passion, Innovation, and Growth.* Newburyport, MA: Red Wheel Weiser/Career Press, 2017.

Chamorro-Premuzic, T. "Why Humble Leaders Are Rare," *Forbes*, June 29, 2020.

Collins, J. *Good to Great.* HarperAudio, 2010.

Dell'Osso, L., P. Lorenzi, B. Nardi, C. Carmassi, and B. Carpita. "Post Traumatic Growth (PTG) in the Frame of Traumatic Experiences," *National Library of Medicine*, 2022.

Deutschman, A. "Change or Die," *Fast Company*, 2005.

Farber, S. *Love Is Just Damn Good Business.* New York: McGraw Hill, 2019.

Goldsmith, M. *What Got You Here Won't Get You There.* New York: Hachette Books, 2013.

"Hunter S Thompson: In His Own Words," *The Guardian*, February 21, 2005.

Lembke, A. *Dopamine Nation: Finding Balance in the Age of Indulgence.* New York: Dutton, 2021.

"Ordinary People Produce Extraordinary Results," *Los Angeles Times*, January 14, 2000.

"Peter Drucker on Marketing," *Forbes*, June 30, 2021.

Peters, T. *Excellence Now: Extreme Humanism.* Chicago: Networlding Publishing, 2021.

Peters, T. J., and R. H. Waterman, Jr. "In Search of Excellence: Lessons from America's Best-Run Companies," HarperBusiness, 2006.

Pressfield, S., and S. Coyne. *The War of Art: Break Through the Blocks and Win Your Inner Creative Battles.* Mission, TX: Black Irish Books, 2012.

Rao, M. "Be Adaptable: Leadership Lessons from Jack Welch," *Training*, June 6, 2017.

Rotella, Bob. *How Champions Think*. New York: Simon & Schuster, 2016.

Tedeschi, R. G., and L. G. Calhoun. "The Posttraumatic Growth Inventory: Measuring the Positive Legacy of Trauma," *Journal of Traumatic Stress*, 1996, 9, pp. 455–471.

Thomson, D. G. *Blueprint to a Billion: 7 Essentials to Achieve Exponential Growth*. Hoboken, NJ: Wiley, 2005.

Warren, R. *The Purpose Driven Life*. Grand Rapids, MI: Zondervan, 2012.

Zander, R. S., and B. Zander. *The Art of Possibility: Transforming Professional and Personal Life*. New York: Penguin Books, 2002.

WEB RESOURCES

Marshall Goldsmith Stakeholder Centered Coaching, *www.mgscc.net*.
Strategic Coach, *strategiccoach.com*.
Verywell Mind, *verywellmind.com*.
Growthink, *growthink.com*.

INDEX

ABOUT THE AUTHOR

Hugh Blane doesn't claim to know everything about your business. He does claim, however, to know a lot about converting human potential into accelerated business results. His consulting firm, Claris Consulting, is retained by a host of high-profile clients around the globe to help them challenge assumptions, jettison complacency, and catapult growth.

Hugh has worked with high-potential employees at prestigious universities and serves as an adjunct professor at the School of Law and Entrepreneurship at Pepperdine University. He has taught business literacy courses to homeless men and women through the Union Rescue Mission in Los Angeles, and has served on the strategic planning committee of the Boys and Girls Club.

Hugh is a serial entrepreneur who doesn't shy away from reinventing himself. After eleven years as CEO of his own financial consulting firm, he was recruited to join renowned business author Tom Peters as a senior-level consultant with the Tom Peters Company. After traveling to three continents and working in seven countries and forty-three states, he left Peters to become the youngest partner and consultant in the venerable consulting firm, The Effectiveness Institute. Seven years later, he knew it was time to reinvent himself again and founded Claris Consulting.

Hugh is the author of *7 Principles of Transformational Leadership: Create a Mindset of Passion, Innovation and Growth* and *Mastering the Leadership Mindset*. He has published over 425 articles and videos on leadership influence and leadership communication. He is a Masters Level Marshall Goldsmith Stakeholder Centered Coach, a Certified Flow Coach with the Flow Research Collective, and a graduate of the Million Dollar Consulting College.

Hugh once ran with the bulls in Pamplona and learned how not to get gored. He is happily married to Alyson, and they love biking, bourbon, and barbeque. They reside in the small beach community of Normandy Park, Washington, with a giant black schnauzer named Remy.

You can learn more about Hugh at his website, *clarisconsulting.net*, or contact him directly at *Hugh@clarisconsulting.net*.